# How to Become a
# Water Walker

## Lessons in Faith

by

Andrew Wommack

Harrison House
Tulsa, OK

Unless otherwise indicated, all Scripture quotations are taken from the King James Version of the Bible.

*How to Become a Water Walker: Lessons in Faith*
ISBN 13: 978-168031-016-0

18 17 16 15                    10 9 8 7 6 5 4 3 2 1

Copyright © 2015 by Andrew Wommack Ministries
850 Elkton Drive
Colorado Springs, CO 80907
www.awmi.net

Published by Harrison House Publishers
Tulsa, OK 74145
www.harrisonhouse.com

# Table of Contents

Introduction

Chapter 1 – The Lord Spoke ............................................... 7

Chapter 2 – He Would Have Passed Them By ........................... 13

Chapter 3 – Be of Good Cheer ............................................ 19

Chapter 4 – Don't Be Afraid .............................................. 25

Chapter 5 – A Word from God ............................................ 33

Chapter 6 – Look for Something More .................................... 39

Chapter 7 – How Are You Asking? ........................................ 47

Chapter 8 – Get Out of the Boat ......................................... 53

Chapter 9 – Take a Step of Faith ........................................ 59

Chapter 10 – Faith Pleases God .......................................... 67

Chapter 11 – Because of Your Unbelief .................................. 73

Chapter 12 – Only Believe ................................................ 79

Chapter 13 – Unbelief Will Sink You ..................................... 85

Chapter 14 – A Pure Faith ................................................ 93

Chapter 15 – Exercise Yourself........................................................ 99

Welcome to Your New Life!

# Introduction

Every one of us has situations in our life that look like they're about to kill us and we need a miracle from God. If that doesn't describe you now, hang on because it will. If you want your life to count for God, you will come into a storm that could kill you before you reach your destination. We have a supernatural God, and if you truly make yourself available, He'll lead you to do things that are far beyond your own natural ability. Therefore, if you are genuinely seeking God, you should have something that you're stretching out and believing Him for.

In a very real sense, that's what Peter and the rest of Jesus' disciples were doing in Matthew 14. They found themselves in a dangerous situation and they needed a miracle. So Peter got out of the boat and walked on water. He did something that no one in all of recorded history—besides Jesus—has ever done!

This story is full of lessons for us today. Peter's example shows us the importance of God's Word, what we can do to maintain our faith once we step out of the boat, how we can avoid sinking, and so much more. By applying the truths contained in this book, you'll radically improve the way you receive from God.

These lessons on faith aren't just for the super-spiritual—this is basic Christianity! Although God wants every believer walking on water, very few are. Instead of trusting Him for a miracle, most Christians cling to the boat seeking their security there. Although the boat is going down fast, at least they have some company. With everyone else sinking at the same rate, they console themselves thinking, *We're all in the same boat!*

Don't settle for what the world is doing. God is calling us to a higher standard of living. Let's step out in faith and walk on water. We'll see greater miracles than ever before!

# The Lord Spoke

## Chapter 1

In Matthew 14, Jesus fed five thousand men with five loaves and two fish. Taking into account the women and children present, there could have been upwards of ten, fifteen, or even twenty thousand people! Then, immediately after this miracle…

**"<u>Jesus constrained his disciples to get into a ship, and to go before him unto the other side</u>, while he sent the multitudes away. And when he had sent the multitudes away, he went up into a mountain apart to pray: and when the evening was come, he was there alone. But the ship was now in the midst of the sea, tossed with waves: for the wind was contrary"** (Matthew 14:22-24; emphasis mine).

Notice how the Word says that Jesus constrained His disciples to get into the ship and go on to the other side. He didn't tell them to go only halfway and then drown. This is important!

## God's Word

These words about going to the other side were spoken by the Creator (Colossians 1:16). Jesus is the one who spoke that very lake into existence. All of His words carried that same creative power. When the Lord says something, there's a purpose for it. He never wastes His breath. He never speaks an idle word. If the Lord has ever told you something, He meant every single bit of it. Everything God says is significant!

These disciples didn't think about whom it was that told them to do this.

**"In the beginning was the Word, and the Word was with God, and the Word was God...All things were made by him; and without him was not any thing made that was made"** (John 1:1,3).

This passage goes on to say that Jesus was that Word.

God spoke everything into existence, and He did it through Jesus. The Lord upholds...

**"All things by the word of his power"** (Hebrews 1:3).

This entire world is held together by the integrity of His Word...

**"And by him all things consist"** (Colossians 1:17).

The God who created everything physical—including the wind, waves, and water they were about to encounter—was Jesus. Jesus was the parent force, and He said, "Get in and go to the other side!" Apparently, the disciples didn't understand who they were dealing with.

## Overwhelmed by Circumstances

The disciples had glimpsed who Jesus was, but they weren't keeping it foremost in their thoughts. Although Peter had confessed a couple of chapters before, **"Thou art the Christ, the Son of the living God"** (Matthew 16:16), he wasn't thinking like that now. As a matter of fact, the Bible says they were shocked to see Him walk on the water because their hearts were hardened. They hadn't considered—meditated, pondered, thought on—the miracle they had just seen.

**"They were sore amazed in themselves beyond measure, and wondered. For they considered not the miracle of the loaves: for their heart was hardened"** (Mark 6:51-52).

If they had really thought about Who this was Who had told them to do this and what He had just done, they wouldn't have been so overwhelmed. This Man had just taken five loaves and two fish and fed almost twenty thousand people. Not only that, there was more left over when everyone was finished than what He began with! If the disciples had been focused on that miracle, they wouldn't have been shocked to see Jesus perform another one. They would have been expecting it. Or they could have taken Jesus' words, believed them, and then stilled the storm or walked on the water to the other side. That's what the Lord wanted them to do.

In the midst of that storm, the disciples could have stood on the Lord's word to them and said, "He didn't tell us to go to the middle of the lake and run the risk of drowningg !" The disciples had already seen Jesus command the wind and waves to cease (Mark 4:39). They could have drawn on that same example and used their faith to calm the present storm as they had seen Jesus do before.

You might say, "But Andrew, this was a severe storm!" Most people would give the disciples a total pass on this and sympathize with them completely. But they weren't the disciples of a mere man, and the instructions they had to go to the other side weren't just powerless words. They had what they needed to accomplish Jesus' instructions. They just reverted to being carnal and forgot all the supernatural lessons they had been taught that day.

The Sea of Galilee is only 7.5 miles wide and 12.75 miles long. I've been there before. We went out on the water in a tourist vessel called "The Jesus Boat" and I taught about the things recorded in the Gospels that happened there. It was a fun experience! However, this isn't a big sea and the disciples' destination was only about four miles away.

## "Why Are You Fearful?"

The disciples boarded the boat and set out from shore sometime around sunset, which could have been anywhere from six to eight o'clock in the evening (Mark 6:47). Yet, here it was in the fourth watch—somewhere between three and six in the morning—when Jesus came to them (Mark 6:48). So in seven to twelve hours they had only covered two miles, or what normally would have been an hour's trip. Most people would say, "Man, you can't fault them. Look, the winds were really bads!" But again, that's because we magnify physical, natural things instead of the God we serve.

When the Lord spoke to the disciples here, He didn't compliment them or say, "Guys, I'm sorry. It's My fault. I shouldn't have left you out on the sea by yourself. I'm responsible. I should have been there and done something." No, that wasn't the Lord's response. He expected them to do better than they did. He expected them to make it to the other side, just as He had instructed them. Likewise, I believe the Lord expects us to do better than most of us are doing. We have His promises. We just aren't believing them.

Many people identify with the disciples and say, "I understand exactly how they felt. It's hard to maintain your faith when you're in the midst of a storm!" Although the Lord understands and has compassion on us, this isn't normal. It may be normal according to those who don't believe God, but this isn't the normal Christian life.

We need to recognize and focus on Who we serve, the command He's given us, and what He's already done. God didn't call you to lose this battle and be a failure. He didn't call you to die of sickness or to live in such poverty that you can't fulfill His will. God made you a world overcomer (1 John 5:4)! You need to start meditating on the promises and words that God has spoken to you. Instead of being overcome by your problems, you would overcome your problems by His promises.

When Jesus spoke to the disciples, He didn't tell them, "Go part of the way. Then, if there's absolute calm, you might make it. But if a storm comes up, you guys have had it!" No, He told them to go to the other side. They had a word from Creator God and if they had put absolute faith in that, they could have stood in the face of that storm and defied it. They could have walked on the water like Jesus and Peter did!

## In Over Your Head or Playing It Too Safe?

This instance of Jesus walking on the water to His disciples is recorded in three of the Gospels (Matthew 14:22-33; Mark 6:45-52; and John 6:15-21). John 6 shows us another important detail.

**"Then they willingly received him** [Jesus] **into the ship: and immediately the ship was at the land whither they went"** (John 6:21; brackets mine).

The disciples and Jesus were translated two miles to the other side! What a miracle! The boat and all its inhabitants were instantly transported to the other side where Jesus originally told them to go. It's very possible that if they had stood and believed, maybe this would have happened for them even before Jesus showed up on the scene.

When God commands us to do something, everything in creation has to bow its knee to what He says. The only reason this doesn't happen is because few people really believe. We get swamped by the storms of life. If we would get this attitude of faith, it would change our experience. If the disciples would've had this attitude, they would have had a totally different experience.

**"But the ship was now in the midst of the sea, tossed with waves: for the wind was contrary"** (Matthew 14:24).

At times, God will tell us to do things that go against the normal flow of nature. God lives in the supernatural realm and if we are truly following Him, we will too. If we aren't supernatural, we're just superficial. The Lord wants us to move into the unlimited, supernatural realm with Him.

The Lord may have laid things on your heart that just seem absolutely impossible. The wind, waves, and storms of life are coming against you and it looks like you could drown. Instead of accomplishing God's will, it appears like you're going to die in the attempt. If you haven't ever been in something like this where you've gotten in over your head, it's probably because you're playing it too safe. Get out on the limb. That's where all the fruit grows. Step out of the boat and start walking on the water!

# He Would Have Passed Them By

## Chapter 2

"And in the fourth watch of the night Jesus went unto them, walking on the sea. And when the disciples saw him walking on the sea, they were troubled, saying, It is a spirit; and they cried out for fear" (Matthew 14:25-26).

Notice how Mark records this:

"And he saw them toiling in rowing; for the wind was contrary unto them: and about the fourth watch of the night he cometh unto them, walking upon the sea, and would have passed by them" (Mark 6:48).

Jesus was up praying on a mountain overlooking the Sea of Galilee. He was in the same storm, so He knew what was going on. It's not like He was indifferent to the disciples' needs. The Lord knew exactly what they were going through because He was going through it too. He was 100 percent aware of their problem!

It's reasonable to guess that the reason Jesus came down and started walking on the water was so that He could rescue His disciples. But even though He drew near to help them, He made as though He "would have passed by them" (Mark 6:48). In other words, even though it seems clear that the Lord came to the disciples' rescue, presented Himself, and even came close enough so that they could see Him, the scriptures say, however, that He then would have passed them by.

Think about this! It seems obvious He was coming to help them. Yet, He didn't just run out there waving His arms and yelling, "Guys, don't panic! It's Me! Here I am to save the day!" The Lord revealed Himself to them, but they had to call out to Him by faith. They had to reach out and make a demand to appropriate His miracle-working power. In other words, Jesus didn't just do it for them. He revealed Himself to them, but they had to tap into what He had on the inside of Him to be able to receive this miracle.

This is a perfect parallel to how God provides miracles for us today. It doesn't matter what your situation is, God knows what you're going through and He's touched with those same feelings.

## God Knows

When Saul saw the Lord on the road to Damascus, Jesus cried out to him saying…

**"Saul, Saul, why persecutest thou me?"** (Acts 9:4).

Saul had never personally persecuted the Lord Jesus Christ when He walked the earth in His physical body. Rather, he was persecuting the post-resurrection followers of Jesus. This shows us how personally our Lord takes things. Whatever you do to a member of the body of Christ, you do it unto Him.

**"Inasmuch as ye have done *it* unto one of the least of these my brethren, ye have done *it* unto me"** (Matthew 25:40, emphasis mine).

The Lord knows what you're going through. He knows your situation—every feeling, every hurt, every need. At times you may think,

*Nobody knows the trouble I have,* and you feel like you have to explain it to God. Yet, the Word says:

**"Your Father knoweth what things ye have need of, before ye ask him"** (Matthew 6:8).

## "Come Boldly!"

The Lord has already been touched with the feeling of our infirmities. He knows exactly what you're going through and will reveal Himself to you (Hebrews 4:15). He never leaves you nor forsakes you (Hebrews 13:5). God is with you to deliver you from whatever situation you're in. But just as He appeared to these disciples and would have passed them by, you have to make a demand on His power. It's up to you to…

**"Come boldly unto the throne of grace, that** [you] **may obtain mercy, and find grace to help in time of need"** (Hebrews 4:16; brackets mine).

Crying out in desperation and pity, saying, "God, don't You love me? Where are You? Do You exist? Do You care?" isn't making a demand on God. If anything, that's tying His hands because you're doubting His Word. You're doubting His promise that He'll never leave you nor forsake you (Hebrews 13:5).

If the disciples were thinking they were going to die, then they were doubting God's Word. Jesus told them to get into the boat and go over to the other side. He didn't say, "Get into the boat and drown trying to get to the other side." They doubted His Word. They weren't aware of how powerful the promise was that He had given them.

We can only speculate what might have happened if the disciples hadn't called out to Jesus. Would Jesus have intervened on their behalf without any response of faith on their part? I don't know, but the Word says that He **"would have passed by them"** (Mark 6:48). It's possible they could've died!

## People Make Choices

People who adhere to an extreme "sovereignty of God" type of teaching really get upset with this truth. They say, "Nothing can happen but what God wills or allows. He orchestrates everything perfectly according to His plan." Wrong! God's Word abounds with examples that contradict this false assumption. (For a more in-depth look at this, please refer to my teachings entitled *The Sovereignty of God*, *God's Not Guilty*, and *Spiritual Authority*.)

God wills…

**"Above all things that thou mayest prosper and be in health, even as thy soul prospereth"** (3 John 1:2).

Yet, people suffer poverty and die all the time of sickness and disease. Also, the Lord is…

**"Not willing that any should perish, but that <u>all</u> should come to repentance"** (2 Peter 3:9; emphasis mine).

However, Jesus Himself said that many would perish through the broad gate leading to destruction and few would enter by the narrow gate to everlasting life (Matthew 7:13-14). God's will does not "automatically" come to pass. What He *wants* and what He *wills* can be thwarted.

Now don't get confused here. I'm talking about God's will for an individual's life. God is so wise and awesome that if Satan blocks His overall plan one way, the Lord will find some other person and eventually get His will accomplished another way. I don't doubt that at all! But on an individual basis, people die whom the Lord did not want to die. It's God's will for them to be healed but, for one reason or another, they don't receive the healing He's already provided. God doesn't will for wars, heartache, tragedy, divorce, etc. to occur. He's not the one who makes these things happen. People make choices.

## Believe God — or Die

It's possible that Jesus would have just passed on by. He revealed Himself, He was there and His power was available, but if the disciples hadn't cried out, He might have kept on going. If they hadn't responded to Him positively and drawn on His supernatural ability one way or another, it's possible they would have drowned.

You may be in a crisis situation and needing God to do something right away. You may be begging and pleading, but if you don't reach out in faith, you might drown. You need to respond positively to God's Word so that it comes alive and stands up on the inside of you. If you don't believe God, He might just pass on by. It's not automatic that you win. You must believe God!

# Be of Good Cheer

## Chapter 3

**"But when they saw him walking upon the sea, they supposed it had been a spirit, and cried out"** (Mark 6:49).

The disciples couldn't believe that Jesus was walking on top of the very thing that was about to destroy them. Jesus was so cool and so in control.

When we're overwhelmed by the storm, it can cause us to miss the Lord and not draw on His supernatural ability. We can't believe that the very thing that is overwhelming us is nothing to God. We miss the fact that He can walk on top of the very problem that's about to drown us. Many times we're looking for the Lord to be as worried and upset as we are. We think He's going to wring His hands and say, "This is a really big problem!" But that's never going to be the response of the Lord!

Some people say, "Oh man, we need to pray! We need lots of people to fast and pray together. It's going to take two, three, or four hundred people on the prayer chain praying because this is such a big deal! If God provides this miracle, all the lights of heaven are liable to dim. I'm not sure that He can actually pull this off!" They may not use this terminology, but they're expressing the same concept. They think God is as overwhelmed as they are.

Jesus is walking on top of the water—the very thing that's overwhelming you. Whatever your situation is, it's no problem for the Lord. Really, it's no big deal!

# No Problem for Jesus

The only thing that makes something a big deal is our unbelief. We tend to magnify how terrible our situation is. However, it would do you good just to look at things from God's perspective and realize that it's no big deal.

Jesus was walking on top of the very thing that was raging around the disciples, and they supposed it had been a spirit (Mark 6:49). In other words, they just couldn't believe that this wasn't bothering God. They couldn't believe that He wasn't struggling the same way they were. Surely, this was some kind of vision coming toward them. It couldn't be real. Jesus couldn't walk on top of water. That's not normal. It's not natural!

God isn't limited the way we are in the physical realm. And yet, many times we really do think He is limited. I've been asked, "Have you ever heard of anybody being healed of AIDS before? I've heard of cancers being healed, but not AIDS." Nothing—absolutely nothing—is impossible with God! Of course He can handle AIDS! But we think, "A million dollars, five million dollars, a house payment, a car payment, whatever. This is just too big—even for God." We expect Him to feel like, "Hey, I just can't pull this off in such a short time. I need more time to do it." God isn't like that. He can walk on top of anything that's about to destroy us. We need to get used to God being supernatural!

Everyone struggles with this. Sometimes we live so much in the natural realm that it just seems like, "God, is there really a way out of this?" There's always a way out—nothing is too difficult for God. Whatever our problem is, Jesus is on top of it. He's not under it. He's not sinking. He's on top of it. This is no problem for Jesus!

# Bothered?

**"For they all saw him, and were troubled. And immediately he talked with them, and saith unto them, Be of good cheer: it is I; be not afraid"** (Mark 6:50).

This verse just shows how completely in control God is. The things that are bothering you aren't bothering God. And if you would appropriate what is yours in Christ, then you don't need to be bothered either. You really don't! Why? Jesus said...

**"Be of good cheer: it is I; be not afraid"** (Mark 6:50).

The Lord was talking to people who may have thought they were going to drown. They could have been up to their necks in water in no time. These guys were sailors. They were not men who were easily frightened. It wasn't because they had become afraid and were fearful over something that wasn't truly a serious situation. In the midst of this crisis situation, Jesus told them, "Be of good cheer—it's Me. Don't be afraid!"

## Same Stuff—Different Wrapper

You might be in a situation right now where you think that there's just no way you can really rejoice until you see absolute deliverance. However, you can get to a place right here in the midst of it where you're of good cheer. "But Andrew, you haven't been where I am!" Although I probably haven't been in your identical situation, the Bible says:

**"There hath no temptation taken you but such as is common to man"** (1 Corinthians 10:13).

If you think that your situation is unique, you're wrong. If you are exempting yourself from the encouragement I'm trying to give

you because you say, "My situation is worse than yours," then you're exempting yourself from the answers you need to overcome. No situation has taken you except what is <u>common</u> to man.

I get the same stuff—it just comes wrapped in a different bow and package! But I've proven in my life over and over again that you can rejoice when there is no reason in the natural to do so, other than faith. You can rejoice when there's no rationale, no proof, no evidence of anything—except your faith!

## "You're a Good God!"

In the early part of March 2001, my wife and I had just returned home from an international flight. We didn't get to bed until somewhere around midnight. Then at 4:15 in the morning, I received a call from my oldest son saying, "Dad, I'm sorry to tell you this, but Peter [my youngest son] is dead." He told me what happened and I said, "Don't let anyone touch him until I get there. The first report is not the last report!"

I told my wife what I had just heard and we prayed. We commanded life back into Peter. Then we jumped out of bed and got dressed. It took about an hour and fifteen minutes to drive from our house to the hospital in Colorado Springs.

On the way in, I didn't know what was going to happen. I had prayed, spoken, and was believing God for a miracle. I knew He had more for my younger son that what he had experienced. He wasn't living in the fullness of God. I knew there was more for him, but at the same time, there are things a person can do to short-circuit the plan of God in his life. So I didn't know what was going to happen.

After Jamie and I prayed, we didn't say very much because we didn't want to speak forth our doubt and unbelief. But finally I couldn't stand it any longer. Unbelief, sorrow, and grief were beginning to get a hold of me. So as we were driving in, I just started saying, "God, You're a good God!" Just like the Lord said in Mark 6:50, I started cheering myself up and speaking against fear, saying, "Father, You're a good God. I want You to know that whether Peter lives or not, You are a good God. You didn't do this. You didn't cause it." And I just went to praising Him.

As I did, I started remembering prophecies that the Lord had given me about my children—things that hadn't happened yet. The Bible says that you can war a good warfare by the prophecies that have gone before (1 Timothy 1:18). So I thought, *Father, if You prophesied this, then he has to live.* So I just started praising God and by the time we arrived in Colorado Springs, I was excited and happy. I was expecting something wonderful to happen.

## Faith Rejoices Before

Peter had been dead for about five hours and had already turned black, but when I walked into the room, my oldest son said, "Dad, within five or ten minutes after I called you, Peter just sat up." They'd already put a toe tag on him. He was stripped naked and put in a cooler. They'd already pronounced him dead and gone—but he sat up!

I talked to the nurse about it and asked him twice if Peter was actually dead. He told me, "Nobody comes in here like that and leaves alive."

"So, was he dead?"

"If this ever happens again, he'll leave in a body bag!"

I suspect that for liability reasons they wouldn't say Peter had died. I don't have a medical certificate to "prove" that my son was dead, but he'd already turned black and hadn't breathed for five hours. I believe

God raised him from the dead. However, before that situation resolved, I was praising God and full of good cheer!

You might be in the same position the disciples were in when the Lord told them to be of good cheer. The storm was still raging. The boat might have even been sinking. It looked like could drown. Everything was still at its worst, but Jesus said, "Be of good cheer. It's Me. Don't be afraid!"

Most people can't be of good cheer until they see their physical problems resolve. Then, when everything works out, they'll be of good cheer. But faith doesn't work that way. You must first get into faith, resist fear, and be of good cheer while the storm is still raging and the ship is going down. Then, afterwards is when you see the miracle. Think about this. If all the Lord wanted was for His disciples to be of good cheer, then He could have stilled the sea first and then their joy would have come. But He told them to be of good cheer before He stilled the storm. That's because they needed to operate in faith to partake of His miracle. He was soliciting a response of faith from them. He's seeking the same thing from us.

Anyone can be of good cheer and overcome fear once the storm stops and the boat is translated to the other side, but it takes faith to rejoice before you know what the outcome will be!

# Don't Be Afraid

## Chapter 4

Are you in the midst of a storm in your life? Is your boat filling up with water fast? Do you feel like you're about to drown? If so, then Jesus is saying to you now...

**"Be of good cheer: it is I; be not afraid"** (Mark 6:50).

If you genuinely understand this truth, it's enough to make you shout! The Word of God will come alive and make you stand up on the inside, and if you stand up on the inside, then eventually you'll stand up on the outside too. That's when you'll see your physical circumstances change. That's when you'll walk on the water!

## Sympathy or Faith?

Once I was talking with a man at church whom I'd been praying with for healing. Although he saw some improvement in his physical body, the main issue was that he had been discouraged and hurt in his attitude and emotions. After listening to my messages over and over again, he finally started to get it. He told me, "I really believe that if I can ever get myself encouraged and stand up on the inside, then I'll stand up on the outside."

I responded, "That's it!"

He was getting a glimpse of it. He wasn't there yet, but he could see it. He was pressing in that direction, and it was just a matter of time before he would see the physical manifestation. Why? Because he was being of good cheer, he was overcoming fear while the storm was still raging.

Most people would criticize us for encouraging a cancer patient by saying, "Be of good cheer. Don't be afraid. The Lord is with you! Why don't you praise God right now for your healing?" They'd say, "Don't you understand the pain this person is going through? The doctor says they're going to die and here you are speaking 'faith.' You're showing no sympathy whatsoever!" They don't understand that once you are calm on the inside, it's just a matter of time before it becomes calm on the outside. Once you receive the answer in your heart, it will manifest itself in the physical realm.

The traditional approach of dealing with people's problems in the church today, however, is to join them in their pit by saying, "You are absolutely justified in being angry, bitter, and hurt. I know those feelings too!" We just get down, wallow, cry, and get as discouraged and defeated as they are in an effort to "comfort" them. Basically, we're trying to sympathize with them. I'm not saying that we need to be insensitive, unloving, or refuse to acknowledge that someone is struggling. But we need to give them something beyond that.

We need to do like Jesus did. Most people today would say, "Jesus was insensitive. How could He tell people who were up to their neck in water and just about to drown **'Be of good cheer: it is I; be not afraid'**? (Mark 6:50) That's unreasonable. Jesus was a 'faith' person. There's no doubt about it!" People would criticize Him for it, but we need more of that. We really do.

# "It's No Big Deal!"

A young woman in our church who had just gotten married went around telling everyone that she wanted a dozen kids. Some people questioned the wisdom of that, but it was her choice. That's what she wanted. She just couldn't wait to become pregnant and have children. Her husband was a minister and they would itinerate up to six months at a time.

One time while she and her husband were ministering at a church, word came back that she was pregnant. We rejoiced because we all knew how much she wanted children. However, when they returned, she went to the doctor and found out it was a tubular pregnancy. Instead of her having a child, the doctor discovered she had cancer and said, "If I don't remove all of your female organs through an operation, you'll be dead within a week. Even with the surgery, you only have a fifty-fifty chance of living. And if you do live, you'll never be able to have children."

She was given a bleak prognosis. At best, her number one goal of being a mother of twelve looked out of reach. Although I'd heard about her prognosis from someone, I was busy laughing, joking, and cutting up after a mid-week service when she came up and tapped me on the shoulder. I turned around and through tears she blubbered, "Andrew, have they told you what happened to me?"

I couldn't turn off my joy and excitement just because of her situation, so I looked right at her and declared, "Cancer is no problem with God! You act like this is a big deal. It's no big deal!"

I might as well have slapped her in the face. She stopped crying, looked at me, and asked, "What are you saying?"

I said, "It's not any harder for God to heal cancer than it is for Him to heal a cold. You could just believe God. You don't have to go without children and you don't have to die in a week's time."

She asked if Jamie and I would come over and talk to her and her husband about this, so we did. I simply told them, "This is only a big thing because you've made it big. It's not hard for God. It's not like this is going to make the lights in heaven dim if you ask the Lord to heal you."

She asked, "So should I continue to go to the doctor? Should I have the surgery?"

"Well, that's up to you. It's your choice. It's not sin if you do, but if they take out all your female organs, you aren't going to have any children. There was only one virgin birth and you aren't going to have another. That's not the way it works. If it was me, I'd just believe God!"

"But they told me I'd be dead in a week!"

"Well, if you believe that, then you need to let them do the operation. There's nothing wrong with that. If that is where your faith is, go for it. But you can believe God. It's not a problem for Him!"

She chose to believe God. Although it's a long story, it's been at least fifteen years and four or five children ago that all this happened. She lived, and she had all her kids through natural childbirth because any doctor who saw her records wouldn't believe she could have a normal delivery. So she's just had all her babies at home. It wasn't a problem!

## "This Is Going to Be Some Awesome Miracle!"

It's not wrong to show compassion toward people who are hurting, but we must go beyond that. We also need to also show faith and encouragement to people. It wouldn't have done any good if Jesus had come out there and said, "Guys, it's terrible. I can't believe what's happening to you. This is big, really big!" He was the only hope the disciples had. If He had magnified the problem, expressed unbelief, and talked about how bad things were for them, they would have been in big trouble. Jesus needed to minimize the situation, magnify God, and show that His power is so much greater than their circumstances. He did that by walking on top of the very thing that was destroying them and saying, "Guys, don't be afraid. Be of good cheer. You ought to be happy because you're about to see one awesome miracle!" When your faith is quickened, you will get excited and say, "God, this is going to be one awesome miracle!"

My faith quickened while I was driving into Colorado Springs that morning my son died. After hearing the report, I prayed and started praising God. All of a sudden, faith rose up and I began to get excited. Part of what I was thinking was, *God, this is going to be some awesome miracle. He'd already been dead for five hours, turned black, and is not breathing. Boy, this is going to be some great miracle!* And it was! But before I actually saw it, I was excited about what God was going to do.

That's what Jesus was telling these disciples when He said, "Be of good cheer!" They could have really been excited and said, "Jesus told us to go to the other side—not to drown. Yet, there is no way in the natural that we're getting to the other side. This is going to be some awesome miracle!"

## Translated

John's account reveals how they were translated to the other side of the lake.

**"And immediately the ship was at the land whither they went"** (John 6:21).

BOOM! They covered approximately two miles and there they were! Instantly the wind ceased and there was a great calm. Most of us would be thrilled, saying, "Wow, that's awesome! Wouldn't it have been wonderful to have been there!" In a sense, that's what Jesus was saying. It hadn't happened yet. The disciples were in the middle of the storm, but the Lord knew they weren't going to drown in the middle of this lake. He knew it was going to work out, so He said, "Guys, rejoice! You ought to get a load of this. You're about to experience one awesome demonstration of My power!"

This sounds totally off the wall to many people because they live so much in the natural that they don't ever get to a place where they rejoice in the midst of a trying situation. Other folks have heard enough teaching on this that they might rejoice through gritted teeth as "warfare," but not from a genuine heart of faith. They're trying to obtain victory, rather than merely enforcing it.

That's okay if that's where you are spiritually. There's a time and place when you must do it that way. But after a while, you've seen so many victories that you're not just rejoicing through gritted teeth. It's not just something you're forcing yourself to do. You can actually get to a place where you are genuinely rejoicing because you just know that something awesome is going to come out of your situation!

## Midnight Praise

**"And at midnight Paul and Silas prayed, and sang praises unto God: and the prisoners heard them. And suddenly there was a great earthquake, so that the foundations of the prison were shaken: and immediately all the doors were opened, and every one's bands were loosed. And the keeper of the prison awaking out of his sleep, and seeing the prison doors open, he drew out his sword, and would have killed himself, supposing that the prisoners had been fled. But Paul cried with a loud voice, saying, Do thyself no harm: for we are all**

**here**" (Acts 16: 25-28).

Paul and Silas were in the Philippian jail. They didn't just pray and sing praises at midnight so they could be delivered. That wasn't why they were singing and praising God. How do I know? When the Lord sent the earthquake, all the prison doors opened and every man's shackles fell off his feet, but Paul and Silas didn't leave. They just kept right on praising.

If praising God to get deliverance had been their motive, they would have left as soon as the earthquake came. But they were actually praising God out of a pure heart of love. They were excited and worshiping the Lord for who He is. They had actually moved into this place that Jesus was talking about. They were of good cheer and not afraid.

Paul and Silas were rejoicing in their relationship with God. They knew He would take care of things, so they just rejoiced. When deliverance came, they didn't even take it. They stayed in jail. And not only Paul and Silas—every one of those unsaved prisoners stayed too. Wow! That was one powerful manifestation of the presence of God to keep all those ungodly people in their prison cells even after they'd been loosed.

## Either Way, You Win!

You can get to a place where you really are of good cheer and not afraid—even while the storms of life are raging around you. It's not just something you're trying to accomplish; you're there. You have good cheer even in the midst of your situation.

If the doctor tells you that you're going to die, just go to praising God and say, "Father, this is awesome! It would be wonderful if I went to be with You!"

We sing songs like, "When we all get to heaven…" but then when the doctor tells us that we're going there, we start crying. Did we really mean what we sang? If you think about this properly, you'd recognize that if you die, you get to go be with the Lord, and if you receive your healing—which Jesus has already provided for you—then you'll have an awesome testimony. Either way, you win!

If you could get your healing to manifest, it would become a great testimony. It could even open up your entire ministry. You could travel the world telling about how awesome God is for this healing. But if you don't see healing manifest, you get to go be with Him. You could be of good cheer and not afraid regardless of your situation and its outcome. Praise the Lord!

For additional encouragement concerning how to manifest your healing, please refer to my teachings entitled, *God Wants You Well*, *How to Receive a Miracle*, and *You've Already Got It!*

# A Word from God

## Chapter 5

If you don't exhibit faith while the storm is still raging, you won't see your deliverance. Many people go through the motions, praising God and saying some of the right things, but they're just wishing and hoping that it's going to work. Yet, they aren't believing. When you truly start believing, you'll find yourself abounding in thanksgiving.

**"As ye have therefore received Christ Jesus the Lord, so walk ye in him: rooted and built up in him, and stablished in the faith, as ye have been taught, abounding therein with thanksgiving"** (Colossians 2:6-7).

The way faith abounds is through thanksgiving. If you don't have a thankful heart, if you aren't being of good cheer in the midst of your storm, then you may have faith but your faith isn't abounding—overcoming—greater than your fears. When you really get into a God-kind of faith, you'll find that you can persist to the point of excitement and joy. I'm not talking about something you manufacture yourself. It comes from God. It's a calm assurance, a peace, and a joy that comes from knowing that God is faithful. He's never forsaken you, and He never will.

Before the Lord performed the miracle these disciples needed, He told them, "Trust Me. Be of good cheer. It's Me. Don't be afraid. Don't you remember who I am? I'm the one who just fed the multitude. I miraculously multiplied a tiny bit of food. I'm the one who has already seen the dead raised, blind eyes and deaf ears opened, and demons cast out. It's Me! Don't you realize Who you're serving? Don't you recognize Who's with you? It's Me!"

You need to recognize who Jesus is on the inside of you. Once you do this, you will not be afraid. You will experience His joy and peace, and you will be of good cheer!

## "Get In and Go!"

Everything we've discussed thus far is essential before you step out on the water. You need to have a word from God. These disciples had a command from the Lord Jesus Christ. They didn't embark out on the sea on their own. It wasn't their will to go across then and there. It was His.

**"And straightway Jesus constrained his disciples to get into a ship, and to go before him unto the other side"** (Matthew 14:22).

"Constrained" means that Jesus had to use some force. He didn't physically grab his disciples and throw them into the boat. However, they did express some type of resistance toward getting in this ship and going across at that time, so Jesus constrained them. He forcefully told them, "Get in and go!"

Why did the disciples resist? Why did Jesus have to constrain them? Many of these men had grown up as fishermen on the Sea of Galilee. This body of water is famous for having storms come down over the mountains that are to the north and east of it. These mountains would hide storms until they crested over the tops. Then the storms would quickly rush down upon the sea. Due to this, you really had to be in tune with what the weather was like.

## The Weather Report

Most of us don't understand this because we discern what the weather is like by listening to a weatherman. We have virtually no acclimation whatsoever. I remember pastoring a little group of ranchers in Pritchett, Colorado, and they would say, "Well, it's going to rain tonight."

I'd ask, "Did you hear that on the weather report?"

They'd say, "No." They just felt the barometric pressure changing and the humidity in the air. Sure enough, it would be exactly as they thought. They'd say, "Boy, that wind is coming out of the north. That means we're going to have a northerner come in." These guys were much better than the weatherman at predicting the weather. After being around them these guys for just a short period of time, I began picking these things up too. I could and was soon able to tell when a winter storm was coming in.

These disciples were far more in tune with the weather than we are today. That's why Jesus had to constrain them. That storm may not have hit yet, but they could see it coming. All the signs were there and it was against their better judgment to be out on the Sea of Galilee at that time. Yet, they went because Jesus told them to.

## Adversity in God's Will

In Matthew chapter 14, Jesus' disciples had a word from God. But that didn't mean they wouldn't have any problems. Remember, the winds were contrary and the disciples were struggling to get to the other side, yet they were perfectly in the center of God's will. They voiced their reservations, but the Lord—knowing full well what they were feeling—

said, "No, you go to the other side. It'll work!"

You can be perfectly led by God and still experience hardship. Satan will come against you. There will be circumstances in your life that will look like you're not going to make it, but this isn't always an indication that you have missed God.

These disciples were doing exactly what the Lord told them to do. He was aware of their situation and was there to help them. However, he didn't just step in and deliver them without their cooperation. The Lord revealed Himself to them but would have passed them by if they had not called out to Him.

It's important for you to realize in your situation if the adversity you're suffering is the result of your own ignorance or disobedience. For instance, Jonah ran away from God. Instead of following the Lord's instructions, he got into a storm that almost cost him his life. But that storm was totally out of God's will. It was something he shouldn't have had to experience.

You need to be honest enough to evaluate where you are. Is the situation, the storm, or the struggle you're in the result of your own rebellion toward God like it was in the case of Jonah? Did you or did you not have a word from Him when you left the shore? Did the Lord tell you to move in a specific direction at this time?

## Paul and Silas

Paul and Silas encountered great adversity in the center of God's will.

**"And a vision appeared to Paul in the night; There stood a man of Macedonia, and prayed him, saying, Come over into Macedonia, and help us. And after he had seen the vision, immediately we endeavoured**

to go into Macedonia, assuredly gathering that the Lord had called us for to preach the gospel unto them" (Acts 16:9-10).

Within just a few days of being in Philippi (a city in Macedonia province), Paul and Silas were beaten and thrown in jail (Acts 16:22-24). Following God doesn't mean that your life is going to be storm-less, jail-less, or problem-less. Although many people teach that if it is God's will, everything will just work out perfectly—that's just not true.

On another occasion, Paul said:

**"For a great door and effectual is opened unto me, and there are many adversaries"** (1 Corinthians 16:9).

God led Paul into Philippi where he was thrown into prison within a short period of time. Just because you're in a storm and it looks like you're about to drown doesn't mean that you've missed God. Don't let circumstances dictate God's will!

## Call Out to God

Did you have a word from God or not? If so, stand on it full of good cheer because He is with you. Don't be afraid. Exhibit faith before you see the final outcome. Faith is seeing the miracle manifest in your heart before you see it manifest in the physical realm. Start praising, worshiping, and rejoicing before you win your battle. Anyone can praise God after everything is taken care of, but it's a Bible principle that you must operate in faith before you see the physical manifestation.

Regardless of your problem, the Lord is there with you. He knows your situation just as surely as He knew the circumstances these disciples were in. He came out there to help them, but He would have passed them by if they hadn't cried out to Him. You need to call out to God.

Don't just sit there in silence and let your problems overtake you. Call out to God!

Don't call out in unbelief like the disciples did when Jesus was walking on the water toward them and they thought He was ghost or something. Don't cry out in frustration, anger, or bitterness. Call out to Him in faith. Make a demand. Draw on the power of God that is available to you. Express your faith and be of good courage. Don't be afraid. Remember Who it is you are serving. Let your faith abound in thanksgiving. When you do these things out of a heart of faith, you're laying the groundwork for the miracle God is about to perform on your behalf.

If you are in a situation that looks like it will overtake you, take courage. Start believing God. Make sure that you've heard from Him and are in the center of His will. Then call out to God in faith and make a demand on Him and His power. Start rejoicing and be of good cheer, even before you see the storm stilled!

## Overcome!

Once you're truly in faith, you can have such a good time in Him that whether your circumstances ever work out or not won't be the issue. You believe God and possess the proof—faith in your heart. You'll want it to work out for other people's benefit as much or more than your own. You'll just want it to be a great testimony to encourage others and bring glory to God!

The Lord loves you and wants you to be a water walker. He desires that you overcome the storms of life instead of being overcome by them. These simple, yet powerful truths will help you do just that.

# Look for Something More

## Chapter 6

The Lord commanded the disciples to cross over to the other side. Therefore, they were there at God's bidding. They had started to obey Him, which is the reason they were in this storm.

Not all the storms we come into are caused by our own ignorance, unbelief, or sin. You can be perfectly led by God and still experience hardship. Satan will come against you. There will be circumstances that make it look like you're going to drown, but this isn't always an indication that you've missed God.

These disciples were exactly where the Lord had told them to be. He was aware of their situation. Jesus came walking on the water to them, but He would have passed them by. He didn't just step in and deliver them without their cooperation. The Lord revealed Himself to them, but would have passed them by had they not called out to Him and drawn on His power in faith.

We must do the same thing. God is with us in the midst of our situation, but we must call upon Him in faith—not desperation, bitterness, frustration, or pity. He's there to help, but we have to call out.

We also need to recognize that the Lord walked on top of the situation that was about to destroy the disciples. God is not overwhelmed with our problems. He's cool. He's on top of it. Nothing is impossible for God!

**"Be of good cheer: it is I; be not afraid"** (Mark 6:50).

Jesus told the disciples to be of good cheer or rejoice before the wind ceased, while their adverse situation was still going on around them. You must operate in faith before you see your deliverance—not afterwards! Most people today call out for help in desperation, pity, anger, and frustration, but not really in faith. How can you tell if you're in faith—true faith? You'll be abounding in thanksgiving, full of good cheer, and not afraid (Colossians 2:7; Mark 6:50).

Now that doesn't mean that if you're struggling with your emotions or you're fighting off some fears that you're totally not in faith. Don't think that! What I'm saying is that you're not yet abounding in faith. If you are still struggling with all of these things, then your faith hasn't been made perfect yet. The good news is that you can overcome that and begin rejoicing in the midst of your problem anyway. In fact, we don't always have to have perfect faith to be able to see our deliverance manifest, yet we should be shooting for abounding faith. We must learn to operate in faith before we see our deliverance—not afterwards!

## Unplug

The Lord told the disciples to be of good courage because it was Him.

**"Jesus spake unto them, saying, Be of good cheer; it is I; be not afraid. And Peter answered him and said, Lord, if it be thou, bid me come unto thee on the water"** (Mattthew 14:27-28).

Remember, the disciples were in this boat, and had spent somewhere between seven and twelve hours trying to get across the Sea of Galilee.

Normally, this entire trip would have only taken about two or three hours, but here they were only halfway across the lake. In the midst of all this, Jesus came walking on the water. They saw Him and cried out in fear. He said, "Guys, be of good cheer. It's Me. Don't be afraid!" Then Peter responded, "If it's You, Lord, bid me to come to You on the water."

This encounter with the Lord affected Peter in a supernatural way. Peter was able to unplug from his own personal dilemma out on the boat, and focus on the miraculous power and ability of God!

In order to become a water walker, you must first get out of "your self." You must unplug from your own personal problems and fear about what's happening to you, and focus on God. You can't become so engrossed in your own problems, and overwhelmed with the impossibilities you are facing, that you lose sight of the Lord and what He can do.

## Success Exposes Unbelief

I used to attend a minister's breakfast every Tuesday morning when I was in town. Fifteen or twenty ministers would take turns standing up and crying about "the good old days." They'd say, "I remember when this and that used to happen here in Colorado Springs, but now it's just a preachers' graveyard. Nothing significant can happen here anymore. If you come to Colorado Springs to build a large church or ministry, you'll leave feet first. No Spirit-filled church can ever grow beyond a hundred members here." They gave instances of those who had tried. Once they attained 100 or 110 people, the church would split or something similar. I listened to them whine about their storms—their problems—for a while without saying anything. Finally, they looked at me and asked, "Well, what do you think?"

I replied, "Guys, in the past week I've seen blind eyes and deaf ears opened. I've personally seen miracle upon miracle. Churches all over are growing. You guys are totally wrong. You're looking at your situation and thinking that the whole body of Christ is like that. You're just looking at yourself! I don't know all the reasons you are struggling, but I can guarantee you that this isn't going on throughout the entire body of Christ. I praise God that I get to travel instead of being stuck here hanging around your constant negativity!"

You can get to the point where you are looking at and thinking about your own situation so much that you forget the miraculous power of God. For instance, there was a young man in that ministers' group who had come to town to start a church. He was talking like he was going to have a mega church in Colorado Springs, but the other ministers just discounted him and laughed at him. Yet, he and I became instant friends because we were both believing God for something big and looking for something more.

When this fellow first came to town, he stepped right in the middle of a very negative situation. While others focused on what had happened in the past and weren't able to see outside the box, he was able to get outside of his limitations and see beyond his own situation. He looked to God and believed Him. Today, this young man pastors a church that serves thousands of people.

## Destroyed or Motivated?

Peter was just as caught up in the situation they were in as everyone else on the boat. However, when Jesus appeared, he started believing God for something greater. He began thinking, *If Jesus can walk on water, then so can I.* He responded positively to the Lord's words, "Be of good cheer. It's Me. Don't be afraid!" Peter believed Christ's words and began to act upon them.

As a result, Peter was able to rise above his present situation. The boisterous wind and surging waves weren't the main issue. Peter realized that God was with him and that His power was available to him. So he began to respond to that and look for something more. If you're going to be a water walker, you must get your focus off of your circumstances and look to God for something more!

Negative circumstances in your life have the potential to either destroy you or motivate you to something better. For example, before Jamie and I started dating, I dated her best friend who was later diagnosed with leukemia. We all believed it was God's will to heal Jamie's best friend when she had leukemia, yet she died. Although this negative situation nearly overwhelmed me, stunted my growth, and stopped me from doing anything for the Lord, I decided to seek Him even more instead. I purposed in my heart that I would see the miraculous power of God.

Like Peter, I looked to Jesus and responded positively to His words instead of just looking at the negative circumstances. We might have lost that time, but I knew that someday I would see the same thing that killed this girl—leukemia—beaten, and I have, many times over! But first, I had to get this attitude that there was more of God available than what I was presently experiencing. Like Peter, I had to choose a different attitude than the rest of the guys in the boat. When Peter did that, he stepped out and walked on the water!

## "There Must Be More!"

While growing up, John G. Lake saw eight of his siblings—four brothers and four sisters—die prematurely due to sickness. For thirty-two years, there was always at least one member of his family who was an invalid. When his young wife took ill and was on the verge of death, Lake cried out to God asking, "Why are You letting this happen?"

The Lord answered, saying, "It's not Me who is letting this happen. You are! This isn't My will. Satan is killing the members of your family prematurely, and it's your responsibility to do something about it. You have the authority to heal these people!"

John G. Lake heard God and believed, and saw his wife raised up. He began a miracle ministry that saw well over 100,000 documented cases of divine healing. At one time, Spokane, Washington, was declared to be the healthiest city in the United States and they credited this to his ministry.

All this sickness, death, and loss could have just overwhelmed and sunk him, but Lake became motivated to seek God and His Word. He declared, "There must be more! I will see the miraculous power of God manifest in my life!" And he did.

## "Trust Me"

That's what Peter did; he trusted God. Jesus appeared and spoke, "Be of good cheer. It's Me. Don't be afraid!" Basically, the Lord was saying, "Trust Me. The power is available." Peter responded positively and started believing for something more. He was able to look past the howling wind and cresting waves. He looked past the things in the natural and focused his attention on Jesus.

Are you able to look past the circumstances in your life? Can you get out of your boat of self-pity and look to the Lord? Are you able to look past your situation and see that God is victorious and well able to give you hope and encouragement? Or are you going to sit there and let the circumstances of life overcome you?

These are questions that must be answered if you are going to walk on water and see miracles in your life. You must first of all lift your head up and start looking for something else. You have to have the hope that there is something more than what you're experiencing. Shake yourself! Get out of the frustration, discouragement, and despair. Decide to overcome. God's power is truly what delivers you, but it's activated by what you choose to believe. Peter wasn't ready to believe God fully at that exact moment, but at least he called out to Jesus and started making a demand on God's power. Will you do the same?

# How Are You Asking?

## Chapter 7

**"And Peter answered him and said, Lord, if it be thou, bid me come unto thee on the water"** (Matthew 14:28).

Although his intent was good, notice how Peter worded this question. Basically, he was saying, "Lord, if You can walk on the water, I can too. I want to do that!" Peter desired to do what Jesus was doing and walk in the miraculous. That was good, but the way he asked this question was incorrect.

There is no other recorded instance in Scripture—or history—of anyone else walking on water. This is it, right here with Jesus and Peter! Moses, Elijah, and Elisha all parted water and walked across on dry ground, but nobody else ever walked on water. Perhaps it wasn't really God's plan for Peter to walk on water. It was certainly possible because the Lord wouldn't have allowed him to come otherwise, but this wasn't necessarily God's best.

If Peter had asked this question differently and said, "Lord, do You want me to walk on the water with You?" it's possible he could have received a different answer. Jesus could have responded, "Well Peter, I'll come to you. Then we'll go to the other side and everything will be just fine."

It's possible that Peter's faith wasn't totally up to walking on the water and enduring all the unbelief that would come from that action. But Peter specifically asked, "Lord, if it's You, bid me come to You on the water." What else could the Lord say? "Don't come. It's not Me." No, it was Him! The way Peter asked this question left Jesus no option for any other answer.

## "Should I Stay?"

It's important how you ask God questions and discern His will for your life. Years ago, when I was still in the Baptist church, I began getting a hold of faith teaching and started sharing it. Of course, I received a lot of criticism for this. Due to the constant conflict, there were many times during those two years that I thought about leaving the Baptist church and just going on with God.

This was back around 1970, when there weren't any independent, Spirit-filled churches around yet. Pentecostal-type churches certainly believed in the Baptism in the Holy Spirit and praying in tongues, but they were anti-charismatic. In fact, they were some of the biggest persecutors of the charismatic church. Therefore, there was nothing except these established denominational churches. Independent, Spirit-filled churches didn't exist back then, and it was a major step to leave your denominational church.

The constant barrage of criticism hindered and hurt me, but I stayed at my denominational church for over two years because of the way I asked God my question. "Lord, do You want me to just leave the Baptist church and let them go to hell? Don't You care? Don't You want me to stay here and minister to these people?"

How else could God answer that question? "Yes, Andrew. Leave the Baptist church and let all the people there go to hell because I don't care about them." Certainly not! God loves Baptists. He loves every one of the denominations. But the way in which I asked my question, the

Lord couldn't tell me to leave.

Looking back on things, I personally believe God was leading me to move on. He wanted me to follow Him into the Baptism in the Holy Spirit, speaking in tongues, the gifts of the Holy Spirit, and miracles. I praise God for all of the good that came into my life through my denominational heritage—and I love the Baptists—but I personally could not go on with the Lord in that particular church environment.

Finally, it got to the point one day that I just asked, "God, do You want me to stay in this church or not?"

Immediately, He answered, "No. Leave." And I left. This was the beginning of a major shift for good in my life. I realized that I had hindered myself from taking this step earlier because of how I had asked my question. You need to be careful how you ask your question!

## None of the Above!

Many years ago, a young man from Oklahoma Baptist University, OBU, became excited after visiting the church I was pastoring in Segoville, Texas. He told me that although he very much wanted to come sit under the Word and let me disciple him, he had a problem. He had prayed and asked God to specifically guide him where he was supposed to go to school. He received a scholarship to OBU. He'd only been there about six to eight weeks when he decided that he wanted to leave all that behind and come sit under my ministry. But he was confused and said, "God, I know You led me to OBU and provided a scholarship for me, but now I feel like You're leading me down to Segoville, Texas. How could You do that?"

He struggled with this for about three months before he came to me and said, "The Lord has answered my question. He told me, 'Out of the two choices you gave Me—Berkley or Oklahoma Baptist University—OBU was better. But if you could have heard Me, I would have told you that I wanted you to go sit under Andrew's ministry instead.'" Basically, God was telling him, "Instead of only saying, A: Berkley, or B: OBU; you should have included C: None of the above!"

This is why we sometimes miss out on hearing God's voice. We say, "God, do You want me to do A or B?" But you ought to also give Him the option of "C: None of the above." Just ask Him, "Lord, is there anything I'm missing?"

## "Come!"

Peter didn't do that. He just said, "Lord, if it's You, bid me to come!" It really doesn't do us any good to speculate what could have or should have happened here. We don't know what God's original plan or intent might have been. Was Peter really mature enough to handle this or not? All we can do is guess. But the way he asked this question left Jesus no room to say anything except, **"Come"** (Matthew 14:29). If you are believing God for something miraculous and are about to take the biggest step of your life, you need to make sure that it's God leading you to do it, instead of you backing God into a corner and leaving Him no other option.

One of my friends is a wonderful guy who has always been totally in love with the Lord and committed to Him. However, earlier in his life he thought that the only way he could really serve God was to be a full-time minister. So he went on staff with a church and poured himself into running a Christian school for a number of years. Although he did excellent work, he went back in the secular world to work a regular job. When I saw him recently, he told me, "Andrew, I was mistaken. I thought the only way I could serve God was to be a full-time minister.

However, I'm happier and more fulfilled now than I've ever been. In fact, I'm actually reaching out and leading people to the Lord from work! God is so good!"

Are you asking God something like, "Do You want me to serve You by being in full-time ministry or not to serve You at all?" Well, if that's the way you phrase your question, God's going to say, "Serve Me." But it's possible that He would prefer you to stay in the business world and serve Him that way. You need to be careful that what you want to step out of the boat and believe for is truly God leading you, and not just you misunderstanding, confusing, and phrasing things in an incorrect way.

# Get Out of the Boat

## Chapter 8

**"And he said, Come. And when Peter was come down out of the ship, he walked on the water, to go to Jesus"** (Matthew 14:29).

Peter had taken his attention off of the howling wind and swirling water—everything that hindering them from making it to the other side—and was looking at Jesus. He was believing that he could do miraculous things. He had asked, and God had given him the command—"Come!"

One word from Jesus is enough to overcome whatever circumstance, situation, or problem is trying to destroy you. One word! And the good news is that we have lots of words in the Bible. Just one word quickened to you—made alive—is enough to overcome any storm, or problem, you may encounter in your life. That's powerful!

Sometimes we think, *I must read volumes of Scripture in order to build my faith. I have to spend fifteen hours a day studying God's Word,* when in fact, just one scripture—one word from God—can quicken our faith. It's not always the quantity that makes the difference, but rather how much that one thing God has spoken to us means.

I've sat beside people in services before who heard the exact same message I did and they may have been a little blessed, but they just went on about their life without realizing how powerful the word they heard really was. Yet, I sat there and meditated on it until that word exploded on the inside of me. That person had the same ability to receive from that word as I did, but it just didn't impact them the same.

## Power in the Word

You might think that the word "come" isn't a very important word. But it was spoken by the Creator—the One who created everything natural, including the water and the wind. That one word had enough power in it for Peter to walk on water. Likewise, the promises God has given you have enough power for you to accomplish whatever He's told you to do.

If God has called you to be a minister, then…

**"Faithful is he that calleth you, who also will do it"** (1 Thessalonians 5:24).

Paul said:

**"I thank Christ Jesus our Lord, who hath enabled me, for that he counted me faithful, putting me into the ministry"** (1 Timothy 1:12).

You'll discover that when God calls you, He's already seen you as faithful or He wouldn't have called you. In other words, the Lord has faith in you. If God has faith in you, then you ought to have faith in yourself. If you would meditate on this, you'd realize that when God called you, there was more to that call than what you may have recognized. If God has faith in you, then you need to put some faith in you and in the ability of God on the inside of you. You can do whatever the Lord has called you to do!

If God has called you to healing and you haven't seen it yet, then look at the Scripture that says, **"By [His] stripes ye were healed"** (1 Peter

2:24; brackets mine). There is more than enough power to overcome whatever problem you may have—sickness, financial, relationship, etc. The Word of God has more than enough power, but you must step out and act on it in faith.

There were twelve guys in that boat, but only one of them walked on water. Every one of them could have done that. Now again, I'm not sure that would have been God's best, but Peter called out and said, "If it's You, bid me come," and the Lord let him. Every one of those disciples could have said this and done the same thing! Yet most people never get out of the boat because of fear. They simply refuse to take that step of faith.

People say things like, "Well, it's normal for us to get sick every fall and winter. You have to expect these things like the flu. As you get older, your health starts deteriorating. You just have to allow for these kinds of things." That's how the world thinks; that's the world's boat!

We sing these songs that say, "Lord, I'm only human. I'm just a man." That's not a very good song for a Christian to sing because we are not only human—one-third of us is "wall-to-wall" Holy Ghost! We need to start believing for something more. We need to get out of the boat!

## "Just Believe God!"

In a very real sense, people in the boat resist those who are stepping out in faith. They say, "So, are you going to just believe God? Are you really going to trust Him to supply your needs? Why not go to the banker and trust him? Are you really going to believe God instead of taking all this medicine?" Now don't misunderstand what I'm saying. It's not a sin to do these things. It wasn't a sin for these disciples to be in the boat and start out to the other side. But when your boat encounters a storm—when the doctor says you're going to die—why would you still keep taking their treatment if it's not working?

A friend of mine recently died of cancer. I don't understand everything involved in his situation, but I do know that he had a melanoma that just wasn't responding to treatment. He had already been through operations and chemotherapy. He'd done all this stuff, but the doctors said it wasn't helping. So I asked him, "Why don't you just believe God?"

"No, I'm going to continue the treatments."

Again, I wasn't close enough to the situation to know exactly what happened, but I remember thinking when he said that, *Why? They aren't doing any good!* The purpose of those treatments is to kill cells. The doctors just hope it's the cancer cells that die, but it also kills healthy cells. These treatments take away your strength and weaken your immune system.

There are some people who are afraid to take a step out of the boat. They're scared of being different. They have to be like everybody else. Yet, everybody else is miserable, suffering, and dying. They're just afraid to get out of the boat. Make a decision to be different. Get out of the boat! Just believe God!

## "How Long Will You Sit There?"

I ministered several times to a certain man who felt like he was supposed to come to Charis Bible College. Every time we talked, he'd say, "I know it's God, but..." and he would tell me about some specific fear he had. This guy had fear about his job, fear about his family, and fear about almost everything else you can imagine. Finally, I just prophesied to him from the story of the lepers at the gate of Samaria.

**"And there were four leprous men at the entering in of the gate: and they said one to another, Why sit we here until we die? If we say, We will enter into the city, then the famine is in the city, and we shall die there: and if we sit still here, we die also. Now therefore come, and let us fall unto the host of the Syrians: if they save us alive, we shall live; and if they kill us, we shall but die** (2 Kings 7:3-4).

At the time, Samaria was under siege by the Syrians. These lepers—along with everyone else in the city—were dying of starvation. Finally, they asked, "What are we going to do? If we stay here, we're going to die. If we go into the city, we'll die because of the famine. Why don't we just get up and go out to the Syrians? If they kill us, so what? But they might feed us—and let us go!"

When the lepers went to the Syrian camp, it turned out that the Lord had caused the Syrians to hear a noise and flee. They left all their tents, gold, clothes, and food behind. Not only were these lepers fed, but they became rich and honored too because they were the ones God used to bring this good news to the rest of the city.

After I told this guy the story of the lepers, I asked, "How long are you going to sit here? Until you die? Take a step of faith in the direction you believe God wants you to go. Do something!"

## Run the Risk

Before you can walk on the water, you have to get out of the boat. You must be willing to depart from what everybody else is doing. You have to be willing to go out and try something new. You must be willing to break with tradition, get out there, and run the risk of failure.

Many people are so afraid of failure that they continue to stay in the situation they're in, which guarantees their failure will continue. If you aren't stretching yourself and believing God for something bigger than what you can produce on your own, you're already a failure. I don't say this to condemn or hurt you, but rather to challenge you.

God is a supernatural God! God is a big God! He is...

**"Able to do exceeding abundantly above all that we ask or think, according to the power that worketh in us"** (Ephesians 3:20).

## Are You Normal?

Is your life "normal" according to the world's system? Can anyone tell the difference between you and your neighbor? Do you go to the doctor as often as they do? Do you have the same number of bills and indebtedness as they do? Do you have the same worries and cares as they do? Does it bother you the same as your unsaved friend when everything negative happens in this world? If so, something is seriously wrong.

You need to believe God for something bigger! There ought to be enough evidence to convict you if you were arrested for being a Christian. There should be something different about you compared to your unsaved neighbor. They're dead and you're alive!

Before you can see that kind of power manifest in your life, however, you need to make a conscious decision to leave the safety of the boat and get out on the water. Before you can be a water walker, you must be willing to step out of the boat. Before you can see the miraculous power of God in your life, you must be willing to run the risk!

# Take a Step of Faith
## Chapter 9

When the Lord touched me on March 23, 1968, He lit a fire in my heart. Even though I had already been born again for ten years, this was when I really got turned on to God. I was in college at the time, and the Lord told me, "Nope, that's not it." God had something bigger for me than being a math major, so He started challenging me to make some decisions.

One of those decisions was to quit school. This meant losing $350 a month in government support from my deceased father's social security. If I stayed in school, I kept the money. If I dropped out, I lost it. This caused fear, worry, and concern because $350 a month for a young single man in 1968 was a decent amount of change. Many people counseled me saying, "That can't be God. You're taking a huge risk!" So why did I do it? I wanted to obey the Lord.

This also took place at the height of the Vietnam War. I had a school deferment as long as I stayed in college, but if I quit, I could expect an all-expense paid trip to Vietnam. This was before they had the lottery system for the draft, so it wasn't based on chance. If you quit school and were a healthy eighteen or nineteen-year-old male, you went to Vietnam. There were no options. I was running the risk of getting hurt, being maimed for life, or even dying. Yet, I went ahead and jumped out of the boat!

I took a step out on the water and began walking in the realm of the miraculous. If God didn't come through, I was sunk! Looking back on it now, those were some of the greatest decisions I've ever made in my entire life. Since then, I've made thousands upon thousands of decisions where it would have been easier to stay in the relative comfort of where I was. But, I wanted to believe God. I longed to follow Him and get out there where Jesus was.

Since you're reading this book, you probably desire to be out there on the water too. You want to be doing something miraculous and making your life count for the kingdom. You long for God's power, but you're afraid to leave the boat.

## Faith Killers

Peter never would have walked on the water if he hadn't first stepped out of the boat. You have to get out of the boat before you can walk on water. You can't walk on water in the boat. You have to get out of your comfort zone. The fear of being different, of running a risk, and the desire to be safe are all real faith killers.

**"Yea, they turned back and tempted God, and limited the Holy One of Israel"** (Psalm 78:41).

You limit God by not having a vision, fearing the unknown, thinking small, fearing change, being unwilling to take a risk, fearing failure, not taking a step of faith, being lazy, and staying in the boat. This limits what God can do in your life. You need to take the limits off God! My teaching entitled *Don't Limit God* will show you how you can do this.

# Out on the Limb

Some people just can't transition from taking the so-called security the world has to offer to getting out of the boat. However, the fruit grows out on the limb! Most of us want to hold onto the trunk and still have all the fruit that comes from being out on the limb, but it doesn't work that way. You need to get out there where you're bobbing up and down in the breeze. You need to feel that insecurity of wobbling around and wondering, *Is this thing going to hold me or not?* That's where the fruit comes.

When you get out of the boat and start believing God for something big, you will start seeing miracles. For me, it's been nearly four decades of stepping out of the boat, and I get excited every time I do something big! I've taken some big steps in my life. I moved from a small 14,000 square foot building to a 110,000 square foot building. We not only took the huge step of buying that building, but we did over $3 million in renovations debt free. While we were doing all of these things, we also doubled our television coverage and more than doubled our staff. This was a huge step out of my boat, and it's not over yet!

I've taken new steps of faith that make those previous steps look small. If the Lord doesn't come through, we're sunk. But I have faith that the best is yet to come. I'll never go back to playing it safe. I'm going for it!

You might say, "Andrew, you shouldn't say that. What happens if it doesn't come to pass?" Well, what happens if it does come to pass? I've seen God come through so many times. I know He's not limited. The only limitation He has is me. So I'm getting out of the boat!

## Afraid of Failure

So what if, like Peter, I don't do it perfectly? What happens if I only walk part of the way? What would happen if only part of my vision comes to pass? What happens if I shoot at the stars but only hit the moon? Some people would look at that as failure. I look at that as still being better than staying earthbound.

We're just so afraid of failure. We're so scared of what other people say about us. Yet, I think the people who are the biggest failures are those who do nothing. If you shoot at nothing and hit it every time, that's a failure!

Peter had to get out of the boat. He had to get beyond his immediate circumstances and start believing God for something bigger. If you want to be a water walker, you have to be willing to get out of the boat. Some people refuse to lose sight of the shore. They won't get in over their ankles. They're afraid of what might be out there.

If you knew the water was only six inches deep, you wouldn't mind getting out of the boat. Why? You'd know what's underneath the surface. However, one of the aspects of truly getting out of the boat is not knowing what's out there. You don't know how deep the water is, so you're dealing with the fear of the unknown. You are probably getting in over your head! But in order to get out of the boat and walk on water, you must be willing to trust the results—the future, the unknown—to God.

## Try Something New

You have to be willing to take a risk. If you're the type of person who wants your whole life planned out and simply refuses to take a risk, then you'll never walk on water. If you insist on knowing exactly where you'll be, what you'll be doing, and who you will be doing it with twenty years from now, you'll never see God's best. It takes faith to see the real supernatural power of God.

A good friend of mine says, "God will usually terrify you before He edifies you!" God's vision for your life will be bigger than what you can do, and it will overwhelm you. My friend also says, "If your dreams and visions don't keep you up at night, you're thinking too small!" If it's God, He'll call you to do something that's beyond your ability. You'll have to get in over your head and run the risk of failure. That just comes with the territory!

Part of being a water walker is being willing to get out of the safety of the boat. You have to depart from what's familiar and what everybody else is doing. You must be willing to try something new. Step out and take a chance!

## Paralyzed

One time, I ministered to a man who was paralyzed. He had been paralyzed for twenty years. I prayed for him and he started moving his legs, yet he wouldn't get out of his wheelchair. He always had an excuse—first this, then that. But in my heart, I knew he was healed.

After several weeks of this, he got back to where he was paralyzed again. Finally, he told me, "I'm afraid of getting out of this wheelchair. I've been in it for twenty years. I used to be a sheriff and became paralyzed when I took a bullet to the spine in the line of duty. If I got up out of this wheelchair and walked, I would lose my disability checks. Plus, people think I'm a hero. They pity me and sympathize with me. I'd lose that too if I could walk. People would wonder if I was ever really paralyzed. I'm secure. I couldn't go out and get another job now. I don't know how to do anything but be a sheriff, and I'm too old to go back to doing that."

This man was only about fifty years old, but he was afraid to get out of his wheelchair because he became comfortable with the money, sympathy, and attention he received. This guy was paralyzed. He was limited. He was missing out on so much of life, but was willing to let it pass him by so he could have money, keep his friends, and have people pity him and sympathize with him. He totally missed the fact that he could have made all kinds of new friends, glorified God, and done things that he hadn't done before. The Lord would have provided for him. Who knows what his future could have been if he had been willing to get out of that wheelchair.

## What Is Your Boat?

This man's wheelchair was his boat. What is your boat? Is your hometown your boat? Are you secure in your hometown and afraid to leave? I'm not saying that God tells everyone to leave their hometown, but He may be calling you to do something where you'd lose the security of your hometown and some other familiar places. If you were to serve God full force, you might lose some friends. You might say, "But what would I do without them?" Wrong question! What are you not doing because of them? Are you willing to let God's will pass you by just because you're afraid to run the risk and step out of the boat?

I lost some lifelong friends when I made a commitment to serve God. It grieved me at the time, but since then God has given me millions of other friends—better friends, closer friends. The promise of the "hundred-fold" return is for those who step out of the boat (Mark 10:28-30). Are you going to be one of those who step out of the boat?

You can see what you're leaving, but not what you're missing. In other words, hindsight gives you the ability to look back and see what it cost you to serve God, but you don't have the ability to look forward and see what you'll be missing if you don't serve Him. God is a good God. He'll never require more of you than what He gives to you. You'll always be more blessed in following the Lord than you ever would in not following Him. But you must be willing to get out of the boat!

*Water Walker*

# Faith Pleases God

## Chapter 10

Peter walked on the water and people criticized him. However, outside of Jesus himself, he's the only person who has ever physically walked on water. Peter may not have done it perfectly, but he did it. I believe God was thrilled when Peter stepped out of the boat and walked on the water—I really do.

**"But without faith it is impossible to please him: for he that cometh to God must believe that he is, and that he is a rewarder of them that diligently seek him"** (Hebrews 11:6).

There have been times when I've failed. I've started trying to believe God and made some mistakes. After going two steps forward, I've had to retreat and take one step back. I've had to lay off staff and cancel radio stations. I've had to back up at times. I don't think it was God's will. I just didn't do it perfectly. I've stumbled and fallen along the way. There have been times when I was late paying my bills. That's not the way the Lord wanted it to be. Praise God, I haven't been late on a bill since the early nineties.

There was a time in my ministry when we struggled. There was a time I failed and didn't represent God accurately. People criticized me and said, "Some Christian you are!" Some people would focus on the fact that I didn't do things perfectly and condemn me. But, I believe God was looking at me and saying, "He might not be doing it exactly right yet, but at least he stepped out of the boat and is trying!"

I don't think the Lord would fault me or come against me for trying to obey Him. I haven't always done things correctly. Sometimes I've taken a word and made a paragraph out of it. Some people would look at that and say, "So, you were just all wrong!" Well yeah, I've missed it and made mistakes—but God loves faith! Without faith, it's impossible to please Him (Hebrews 11:6). Faith is what pleases God. Even though I may have failed at times, the Lord just encouraged me and urged me on!

I remember when my kids were learning how to ride a bicycle. It took a few tries before they really got the hang of it. They made some mistakes along the way. It would be wonderful if they could just get on a bicycle and ride it perfectly—never wobbling and do everything right on the first try—but most children don't do that. Due to fear, most of them will wobble, fall, and maybe even hurt themselves. But their father gets them up, encourages them, and says, "You can do it! It's not that bad. I fell off my bike when I was learning to ride also."

As a loving parent, you just encourage your children to keep at it until eventually they master the skill of riding a bike. All along the way, you just look at them and encourage them saying, "I'm proud of you for trying!"

Our heavenly Father is more like this than we suspect. When Peter began to sink, instead of God saying, "You didn't do it perfectly. You failed. You didn't walk all the way to Jesus. You only got twenty yards!" I believe the Lord exclaimed, "Peter actually walked on water!" Peter did something that no other physical human being besides Jesus has ever done. I believe God was impressed! He was thrilled to see His son out there trying! Even though Peter failed and started to sink, God was pleased.

# Get Up and Try Again

You may fail. When you get out of the boat, you run the risk of sinking. Peter didn't go all the way under the water, but he began to sink (Matthew 14:30) and Jesus had to rescue him. The good news is that God delivered Peter. He didn't just push him down under the water saying, "You sorry thing. Your faith failed! You didn't keep believing Me. How dare you!" No! Instead of letting him sink, the Lord reached out and lifted him up by his hand.

If you fail, Jesus will be there. Even though people may be hard on you and say, "Well, you didn't do things right," Jesus will encourage you to keep trying. He'll say, "I'm so proud of you. Go for it! Get up and try again!"

If you want to walk on water, you have to get out of the boat. You have to do something. If you fail, the Lord won't fall off His throne. The kingdom of God isn't going to totally rise or fall based on your success or failure. If you fail believing God, you're still a success. You tried. You got out of the boat. You walked on water.

If you're doing it out of your own presumption because you aren't waiting on God, His way, and His timing—that's a different situation. But if you're doing it out of a pure heart and can truthfully say, "Father, I'm doing this because I believe with all my heart that this is You leading me to take a step of faith, trust You, get out of this boat, and move in this direction," then go for it! If you fail, you won't fail. You'll be a success in God's eyes!

# Follow His Leading

When we stand before God and He judges us for what happened in our lifetime, I believe we'll be surprised. He's going to look at some people whom the world considered failures and say, "You stepped out in faith and were trying to obey Me." Faith is what pleases God!

The Lord is more pleased with faith than He is with "success." If you could somehow or another "succeed" without trusting God, you've failed. You could have money, prestige, honor, recognition, possessions, and influence, but if you haven't really trusted God and stepped out to do what He wanted you to do, then you've failed. You might be considered a great success in the eyes of men, but God will look at you and say, "You failed to do what I told you to do."

On the other hand, there will be people who didn't amount to much in the eyes of the world. They didn't have much, yet they trusted God. They believed Him and did what He told them to do. The Lord will say to them, "You good and faithful servant!" God never bases His opinion of faithfulness only on the outcome, but rather on whether or not you were following His leading. That's encouraging!

If you want to walk on water and see the miracle power of God manifest in your life, get out of the boat and trust God. If you fail, you've learned something. Jesus will pick you up. And if the Lord tarries, someday two thousand years in the future, people will be talking about how you trusted God. You'll be an inspiration to somebody else the way Peter is to us. If Peter had stayed in the boat, we wouldn't be discussing him walking on water. This chapter in the Bible wouldn't have been there. Praise God that somebody had enough faith to trust God. Although he failed, I admire Peter for being able to look beyond himself, get out of the boat, step out there on the water, and trust Jesus.

That's awesome!

Do you want to walk on the water? Make a break! Get out of the boat! Do something!

*Water Walker*

# Because of Your Unbelief

## Chapter 11

"**And when Peter was come down out of the ship, he walked on the water, to go to Jesus**" (Matthew 14:29).

In order to walk on water, you have to get out of the boat. You must leave the comfort and security of whatever you're in and take a risk. Depart from the norm. Separate yourself from the crowd. Do something! Everybody wants to walk on water, but nobody wants to get out of the boat.

"**But when he [Peter] saw the wind boisterous, he was afraid; and beginning to sink, he cried, saying, Lord, save me. And immediately Jesus stretched forth his hand, and caught him, and said unto him, O thou of little faith, wherefore didst thou doubt? And when they were come into the ship, the wind ceased. Then they that were in the ship came and worshipped him, saying, Of a truth, thou art the Son of God**" (Matthew 14:30-33; brackets mine).

"**And the sea arose by reason of a great wind that blew. So when they had rowed about five and twenty or thirty furlongs, they see Jesus walking on the sea, and drawing nigh unto the ship: and they were afraid. But he saith unto them, It is I; be not afraid. Then they willingly received him into the ship: and immediately the ship was at the land whither they went**" (John 6:18-21).

This is one reason why you need to take all of the Gospels' accounts on one story and put them together. Matthew alone shows Peter making this request of Jesus and walking on the water. John alone shows that when Jesus entered into the ship, not only did the wind cease, but the ship and all of its occupants were immediately translated to the other shore. Mark recounts some things Jesus said about hardness of heart. If you just took Mark's account, you wouldn't know that Peter walked on the water and that the boat was translated with the occupants to the other shore. Even though the events still would have been very miraculous, you would have missed some of this information. You get a little different slant from each Gospel. In order to get the full story, you need to put it all together.

## The Natural Realm

Peter got out of the boat and walked on the water. But Matthew 14:30 specifically says:

**"But when he saw the wind boisterous, he was afraid; and beginning to sink, he cried, saying, Lord, save me."**

Peter saw the boisterous wind, was afraid, and started to sink. What did the wind being boisterous have to do with Peter walking on the water? The thing (the wind for example) that took his attention away from Jesus and caused him to begin to sink was a non-essential. It really didn't have anything to do with it. If Peter had kept his eyes on Jesus, the Author and Finisher of his faith (Hebrews 12:2), he would have walked on water all the way to the Lord. Then he could have walked with Jesus back to the boat, or the shore, or anywhere else he wanted to go. He had already proven that he could walk on water. He had already defied the laws of nature. He was walking by faith. The wind and the waves didn't have anything to do with him walking on the water. In the natural, he couldn't have walked on the water if it had been a perfectly calm day. The wind was just something that took his attention away from Jesus.

When Peter took his eyes off of Jesus and began to look at the wind and the waves, he started focusing on the natural realm. Then the natural realm probably began to flood his senses with thoughts like, *You shouldn't be here. This is crazy. You can't do this.* We've all been taught not to get out on a lake and try to walk on water. Peter had also spent his whole life learning that you had better stay in the boat so when he saw the wind and the waves, it brought all these things back to his remembrance and caused him to doubt.

## "Little Faith"

When Peter cried out, "Lord, save me," Jesus immediately...

**"Stretched forth his hand, and caught him, and said unto him, O thou of little faith, wherefore didst thou doubt?"** (Matthew 14:31).

Notice how Jesus said that Peter had "little faith." Most people believe that to do something really miraculous, you have to have big faith, great faith, or tons of faith. But the Lord said Peter had little faith. Yet, as long as little faith was focused on Jesus, it was enough to walk on water.

**"O thou of little faith, wherefore didst thou doubt?"** (Matthew 14:31).

Jesus brought up an important truth here that most Christians haven't really understood, because they're too busy trying to build their faith and come up with a "big" faith. However, the key to the Christian life isn't "big" faith, but rather "little" unbelief.

# Meet the People's Needs

When Jesus and three of His disciples had just come down from the Mount of Transfiguration, there was a man who had brought his demonized son to Jesus to cast the demon out. Since the Lord was up on the mountain with Peter, James, and John, this man requested the other disciples to cast the demon out. They tried, but couldn't.

**"And when they** [Jesus and the three disciples returning with Him] **were come to the multitude, there came to him a certain man, kneeling down to him, and saying, Lord, have mercy on my son: for he is lunatic, and sore vexed: for ofttimes he falleth into the fire, and oft into the water"** (Matthew 17:14-15; brackets mine).

The word "lunatic" means that the boy had some type of a seizure. While convulsing the boy, the demon would throw him into the fire and into the water. Most scholars believe this is talking about something like epilepsy.

**"And I brought him to thy disciples, and they could not cure him. Then Jesus answered and said, O faithless and perverse generation, how long shall I be with you? how long shall I suffer you? bring him hither to me"** (Matthew 17:16-17).

Jesus didn't say, "Guys, I'm sorry. This isn't your responsibility. You don't have the power to deal with this. I should have been here for you. Don't feel bad about it." Not at all! Instead, the Lord replied…

**"O faithless and perverse generation"** (Matthew 17:17).

He rebuked them saying, "How long am I going to be here?" In other words, Jesus wanted His disciples to be able to carry on His ministry.

Today, the Church doesn't feel any conviction about not meeting the needs of our society. We send people who come to us with mental problems to a psychiatrist or a mental ward. We send people with sickness to a doctor. We send people with financial problems to a banker or the government for welfare. However, God intended for the Church to meet the physical, social, and emotional needs of people. God is not pleased today with the Church's inability to do this. If Jesus was here in His physical body, He would be saying the same thing, "You're supposed to be healing the sick, cleansing the lepers, and raising the dead. You don't have to send people to psychiatrists and welfare. You ought to be meeting the needs of people!"

## Why Didn't It Work?

**"And Jesus rebuked the devil; and he departed out of him: and the child was cured from that very hour. Then came the disciples to Jesus apart, and said, Why could not we cast him out?"** (Matthew 17:18-19).

Now this is a very important question the disciples asked. In Matthew 10, the disciples had already received a commission from the Lord. He had given them authority and power over all unclean spirits to cast them out. The disciples went out, came back, and didn't ask any questions like "Why didn't it work?" or "How come this didn't happen?" The absence of a question implies that they'd seen 100 percent success. But here in Matthew 17, they did the same thing they had done before, but without the same results.

Have you ever prayed for something that you really believed was God's will, but didn't see it come to pass? Perhaps you've seen yourself or someone else healed or set free before, but this time it didn't manifest. Due to this, you have a specific quandary because you know what you believe. You've seen that faith work before, but this time you did everything you knew to do as far as you could tell, but didn't get the right results.

It's significant to point this out because there are some people who just don't believe that God does miracles today. Those people aren't asking, "Why didn't it work when I prayed," because they didn't expect God to move. The believers who are the most upset and susceptible to condemnation or feelings that God failed them are those who know that faith works, have believed, or have seen others set free. Yet, this time they did the same thing and didn't see anything come to pass. Therefore, this question—and Jesus' answer—are both very important.

**"Jesus said unto them, Because of your unbelief"** (Matthew 17:20).

Jesus didn't say, "It's because you don't believe" or because of your "little faith" (as the NIV and others incorrectly translate it). That's what most people believe. They think, *Well, wait a minute. If they prayed for something and didn't see it come to pass, it's because they didn't have any faith or their faith was too small.* That's not what Jesus said. You can believe and yet have unbelief at the same time.

# Only Believe

## Chapter 12

"**And they brought him** [the demonized boy] **unto him** [Jesus]: **and when he saw him, straightway the spirit tare him; and he fell on the ground, and wallowed foaming. And he asked his father, How long is it ago since this came unto him? And he said, Of a child. And ofttimes it hath cast him into the fire, and into the waters, to destroy him: but if thou canst do any thing, have compassion on us, and help us**" (Mark 9:20-22; brackets mine).

This father was beginning to despair. His faith was starting to wane. He said, "**IF** You can do anything..." He was beginning to doubt that the deliverance he desired would happen.

"**Jesus said unto him, If thou canst believe, all things are possible to him that believeth**" (Mark 9:23).

This man must have had some strong faith to have brought his demonized son to Jesus. If he hadn't been believing for something, he wouldn't have gone to all this effort. Apparently, this boy was so demonized that he was hard to control. He fell on the ground, wallowed, and foamed at the mouth. This father came expecting something, but "**hope deferred maketh the heart sick**" (Proverbs 13:12). After seeing the disciples unable to cast the demon out, the boy falling down and beginning to wallow and foam, and Jesus asking how long he'd been that way, this father was beginning to waver in his faith.

Basically, this man was putting the responsibility back on the Lord when he said, "Jesus, if You can do anything…"The Lord turned it right around and put the responsibility back on him, saying…

**"If thou canst believe, all things are possible to him that believeth"** (Mark 9:23).

## Faith and Unbelief

Notice the father's response:

**"And straightway the father of the child cried out, and said with tears, Lord, I believe; help thou mine unbelief"** (Mark 9:24).

This is significant! The man said, "I have faith, but I also have unbelief. Lord, help me get over my unbelief!" Jesus didn't counter him by answering, "Now, wait a minute. If you have faith, then you don't have any unbelief. And if you have any unbelief, then you don't have true faith." No, apparently you can have both faith and unbelief at the same time!

The healing of Jairus' daughter reveals the same truth. As the Lord was going to minister to her, He was interrupted by the woman with the issue of blood. He ministered to the woman and she was completely healed. But…

**"While he yet spake, there came from the ruler of the synagogue's house certain which said, Thy daughter is dead: why troublest thou the Master any further? As soon as Jesus heard the word that was spoken, he saith unto the ruler of the synagogue, Be not afraid, only believe"** (Mark 5:35-36).

Why would Jesus tell him to "only believe" if believing automatically excludes doubting? Because you can believe and doubt at the same time! This is why the Lord said:

**"For verily I say unto you, That whosoever shall say unto this mountain, Be thou removed, and be thou cast into the sea; and shall not doubt in his heart, but shall believe that those things which he saith shall come to pass; he shall have whatsoever he saith"** (Mark 11:23).

Jesus told us to believe, speak in faith, and then doubt not in our heart. In other words, we can believe and disbelieve at the same time.

## Pure Faith—Minus Unbelief

Now that's a concept many people don't have. Most Christians don't even take into account the negative effect of unbelief. They just think that the antidote to unbelief is faith. If they recognize the presence of any fear or doubt in their life, they just try to increase their faith. They attempt to overcome their unbelief with more and more faith. But that's not what the Lord was saying. He told the disciples, **"If you believe and doubt not"** (Mark 11:23). To Jairus, He instructed, **"Only believe"** (Mark 5:36). And the father of the demonized boy said, **"Lord, I believe, but help my unbelief"** (Mark 9:24). These are all examples of how you can have faith and unbelief at the same time.

Unbelief is a negative counterbalancing force that cancels out faith. If you hitched a horse up to a weight, that horse could exert enough strength to move it. But if you had a horse of equal strength hitched up and pulling in the opposite direction, then the two horses would negate, counteract, and counterbalance each other. The net effect on the weight would be zero.

In Matthew 17, the reason the disciples couldn't cast this demon out wasn't because they didn't have faith. They did have faith. That's why they were asking the question. However, Jesus told them that the problem was their unbelief, which counteracted and negated their faith.

**"And Jesus said unto them, Because of your unbelief: for verily I say unto you, If ye have faith as a grain of mustard seed, ye shall say unto this mountain, Remove hence to yonder place; and it shall remove; and nothing shall be impossible unto you"** (Matthew 17:20).

Jesus declared, "It's because of your unbelief!" Then He continued saying, "If you have faith like a grain of mustard seed." Since a mustard seed is very tiny, the Lord was basically saying, "You don't need huge faith! If your faith is as big as a mustard seed, it's enough to see a mountain cast into the sea. You just need a pure faith minus unbelief!"

## Confused

Most Christians have the false concept that unbelief is something you can't really deal with. It's just there and all you have to do is increase your faith level to overcome it.

Imagine two thermometers. One is a faith-ometer and the other is an unbelief-ometer. We need to constantly monitor both of these meters. Most people don't even acknowledge, quantify, or gauge the amount of unbelief in their lives. They just think that having fear, worry, stress, or being hurt and falling apart when the doctor tells them they are going to die is just normal. They don't even think about this or do anything to deal with their unbelief. They just try to increase their measure of faith. So they'll read the Word more, pray more, and do other things in an effort to increase and build more and more faith.

This is contrary to everything Jesus was teaching. He said, "If you have faith as a grain of mustard seed, it's enough to cast a mountain into the sea. You don't need a huge faith. You just need a faith that isn't diluted, counterbalanced, and negated by unbelief."

I'm sure you've probably seen faith work. You've seen God answer your prayers, heal you, deliver you, or do something for you or someone you've prayed for. Then you come along and pray for someone else, expecting the same results, but don't see it. It's really confusing because you know you have faith, but do you have unbelief?

Not long after I'd seen my first person raised from the dead, I remember being so excited! I not only believed in theory that God could do miracles, I saw it happen and I was pumped! While holding a meeting in Omaha, Nebraska, I noticed a man in a wheelchair sitting to my left in the front row. I could hardly wait to get through preaching so I could go over there and see him come out of that wheelchair. I reasoned, *If you could see a man raised from the dead, then surely you could see someone come out of a wheelchair.* So I went over and grabbed this guy by the hand and declared, "In the name of Jesus, rise up and walk!" I yanked him up out of that chair and he fell right over on his face. Since he was paralyzed, he couldn't even brace himself to break the fall.

When that happened, people gasped. You could hear their groans. I groaned too. You could actually hear the unbelief. It was tangible, and I didn't know what to do. So I bent down on my knees, took hold of this man, hugged him, wrestled him back into his wheelchair, and said the scriptural equivalent of, **"Depart in peace, be ye warmed and filled"** (James 2:16). But I didn't give him what he needed.

I returned to my hotel room that night confused, saying, "God, I don't understand." What made it so bad was that I had truly expected that man to be healed. I knew I had faith for him to be made whole. You don't just grab a paralyzed guy out of a wheelchair in front of lots of other people and pull him up unless you fully expect him to get up and walk. If I'd ever thought about him falling flat on his face, I wouldn't have done that. I knew I had faith. That's what confused and hurt me so much. If I hadn't had faith, but had been in fear and thinking, *Oh God, I know this isn't going to work, but I'll do it anyway*, then I wouldn't have been surprised. However, I was surprised because I wholeheartedly expected him to be able to walk. I just couldn't understand why this happened. It took me approximately three years to learn some things before I understood why this happened. Most of what the Lord taught me about this is included in my teaching called *Hardness of Heart*.

# Unbelief Will Sink You

## Chapter 13

While reading a book about Smith Wigglesworth, I discovered that he used to start his miracle services by boldly declaring, "The first person to come up here on the stage will be healed of whatever you have!" Someone would come up, he would pray for them, see them healed, and then preach about how it happened. Then he would give an altar call, go through and lay hands on people, and see many, many folks healed. Wigglesworth saw lots of great miracles this way.

At one of Wigglesworth's meetings, two ladies brought an elderly friend who was suffering from a cancerous tumor. As soon as he said, "The first person up here gets healed," they rushed their friend up to the stage. The tumor on this woman was so large that it made her look like she was nine months pregnant. She was so weak that she couldn't stand without her two friends' assistance. They stood on the stage, one on each side of this lady, holding her up. Smith looked at them and said, "Let her go."

They answered, "We can't let her go. She'll fall."

Wigglesworth raised his voice a little and told them, "I said let her go." They did and she fell forward on top of that tumor, groaning out loud in pain. The people in the crowd began to gasp and moan—exactly like when I pulled that man out of the wheelchair and he fell on his face.

Smith Wigglesworth didn't have any more faith when he ministered to that woman than I did when I ministered to that man (Romans 12:3).

The difference was Wigglesworth had less unbelief. When I prayed for that man in the wheelchair and he fell flat on his face, I responded in confusion, shame, guilt, and fear. I grabbed him and helped him back up into his wheelchair. Smith just kept right on going and said, "Pick her up."

They picked the woman up and stood her in front of Wigglesworth again. He said, "Let her go."

The two women responded, "We can't let her go. She'll fall again!"

Wigglesworth yelled at them, "I said let her go!" They did, and she fell flat on that tumor again. He said, "Pick her up." They did. Then he told them, "Let her go." They answered, "We will not let her go!"

Smith barked, "I said let her go!" At this point, a man in the audience stood up and declared, "You beast! Leave that poor woman alone!"

Smith got mad and hollered, "I know my business. You mind your own!" Then he turned to the women and ordered, "You let her go!" They did, and that tumor fell out of her dress onto the stage, and the woman walked off totally healed.

Wigglesworth didn't have any more faith than I did, he just had less unbelief. Can you see the difference?

## Trusting in God

When Jesus' disciples asked, "Why couldn't we cast the demon out," Jesus answered, "Because of your unbelief!" The reason they asked this question in the first place was because they truly believed and were expecting. They'd seen their faith work on other people, but they didn't see the desired results this time. The Lord told them, "Guys, it's not because you didn't have faith. If your faith is only the size of a mustard seed, it's sufficient. You don't need huge faith. Just deal with your unbelief!" This is what most Christians aren't doing. They aren't dealing with their unbelief.

Faith is simply trusting in God. It is having thoughts, feelings, and emotions that are consistent with the Word of God. The Lord said, "You can lay hands on the sick and they shall recover." If you say, "I can do that. I'm going to do that," and start seeing it on the inside, getting excited about it, and then act on it—that's faith.

Unbelief is the opposite. Unbelief is thoughts, feelings, emotions, and actions that are opposed to what God's Word says. Most Christians aren't doing anything to deal with this negative force of unbelief. They're just trying to increase their faith.

People often come to one of my meetings, hear me talking faith, see miracles, and go right home and try to do the same thing. Then they get frustrated and disappointed when they don't get the same results. When I talk to them, they tell me that they go to a church that doesn't even believe in the Baptism in the Holy Spirit and speaking in tongues. Instead of preaching on faith, their church emphasizes this false doctrine commonly called "the Sovereignty of God," which says, "Maybe God made you sick to teach you a lesson." They're around all this unbelief, but don't even take that into account. They think they can just go back, speak the Word, and everything will work. Even Jesus —who always operated in faith perfectly—couldn't do many mighty works in His hometown due to the people's unbelief. The atmosphere of unbelief in a given area or group of people can affect even someone who is operating in faith perfectly.

**"And he could there do no mighty work, save that he laid his hands upon a few sick folk, and healed them. And he marvelled because of their unbelief"** (Mark 6:5-6).

It's not just a matter of the power you exert, but it's also a matter of all the negative things around you. That's why when Jesus raised Jairus' daughter from the dead, He only allowed the father, mother, and a couple of disciples to come in. He put out all the people who were mocking, scorning, and laughing at Him.

**"And, behold, there cometh one of the rulers of the synagogue, Jairus by name; and when he saw him, he fell at his feet, And besought him greatly, saying, My little daughter lieth at the point of death: I pray thee, come and lay thy hands on her, that she may be healed; and she shall live. And Jesus went with him; and much people followed him, and thronged him."** (Mark 5:22-25)

**"While he yet spake, there came from the ruler of the synagogue's house certain which said, Thy daughter is dead: why troublest thou the Master any further? As soon as Jesus heard the word that was spoken, he saith unto the ruler of the synagogue, Be not afraid, only believe. And he suffered no man to follow him, save Peter, and James, and John the brother of James. And he cometh to the house of the ruler of the synagogue, and seeth the tumult, and them that wept and wailed greatly. And when he was come in, he saith unto them, Why make ye this ado, and weep? the damsel is not dead, but sleepeth. And they laughed him to scorn. But when he had put them all out, he taketh the father and the mother of the damsel, and them that were with him, and entereth in where the damsel was lying. And he took the damsel by the hand, and said unto her, Talitha cumi; which is, being interpreted, Damsel, I say unto thee, arise. And straightway the damsel arose, and walked; for she was of the age of twelve years. And they were astonished with a great astonishment. And he charged them straitly that no man should know it; and commanded that something should be given her to eat"** (Mark 5:35-43).

When Elijah, Elisha, and Peter raised people from the dead, they all sought seclusion (1 Kings 17:17-24; 2 Kings 4:32-37; Acts 9:36-41). They separated from the unbelievers and got rid of unbelief. It's the same principle. They had faith, but they didn't want any unbelief around to counter their faith.

## Deal with Unbelief

I meet people constantly who don't even consider the unbelief of others. They just want to go marching in to a hospital and see someone raised up. They don't take into account that everybody there doesn't believe in these things, but instead are resistant and critical toward them. Therefore, we must take into account the unbelief of other people.

Bethsaida was one of the most unbelieving, resistant places to the Lord's ministry of anywhere He'd been.

**"Woe unto thee, Bethsaida! for if the mighty works had been done in Tyre or Sidon, which have been done in you, they had a great while ago repented, sitting in sackcloth and ashes"** (Luke 10:13).

When Jesus encountered a man who was blind there, He had to take him by the hand and lead him away from all of this unbelief. Even when He had the man out of town, He knew He hadn't gotten "all of the town" out of the man. Jesus had to pray for him twice. This is the only time in Scripture that Jesus prayed twice for someone. Finally, once the man saw clearly, Jesus told him not to go back into that town or tell about his healing to anyone in it because of their unbelief (Mark 8:22-30).

Very few people are doing much to deal with unbelief. They're just trying to be strong in faith. However, we need to recognize that just as faith comes by hearing the Word of God, unbelief comes by hearing things contrary to the Word of God. If we are going to be really strong and see our faith produce, we need to cut off the inroad of unbelief into our lives. We simply cannot allow the sewage of this world to flow through our minds and emotions without it affecting our unbelief levels. Unbelief comes through hearing things opposed to God's Word, just like faith comes by hearing things that are in agreement with God's Word.

## Looking Unto Him

As long as Peter looked to Jesus, the Author and Finisher of our faith (Hebrews 12:2), he walked on water. But when he took his eyes off the Lord, he began to see the wind and the waves. Although the wind and the waves weren't demonic or evil, they were contrary to faith.

At times, a breeze can be a wonderful thing. It can cool you off and be very pleasant. Waves aren't bad either. It's actually very soothing to sit on the shore and see waves. However, it's different when they're extreme. The howling wind and tall waves overwhelmed Peter with unbelief. He probably started thinking thoughts like, *I shouldn't be out on this water. I need to get back into the boat!* Most likely if he started having these thoughts, that's when he began to sink.

Notice how Peter didn't just plop down all at once and instantly sink. The Word says that he *began* to sink (Matthew 14:30). Likewise, unbelief doesn't come all at once. It doesn't just jump on you like a seizure. Like faith, unbelief comes gradually through the way you think. You must build and grow yourself in this area. Peter didn't just lose his faith and start operating in unbelief all at once. It was something that happened gradually.

Peter had enough sense to turn to Jesus and call out for help. He could have called back to the guys in the boat. He could have just totally given up all faith whatsoever and thought, *This is crazy. This must not be Jesus. This must be a vision. What am I doing out here?* Peter could have yelled for the guys in the boat to throw him a rope, but instead he turned back to Jesus.

There is no indication that Jesus carried Peter back to the boat. The Word implies that they walked back together. Peter walked on the water again, but this time hand in hand with Jesus and looking unto Him.

## What Are You Thinking?

Lack of faith didn't cause Peter to sink—unbelief did. He began to sink when he took his eyes off Jesus. The reason most Christians never walk on water is because they aren't really looking at Jesus the way they should. If they start walking in a miracle but struggle and begin to sink, it's because they have taken their eyes off Jesus. They are considering what the banker, doctor, family member, or checkbook is saying instead of what God's Word says. They have started thinking about something else. It's not that they don't have faith; it's just that their faith is being negated and counterbalanced by their unbelief that is pulling in the opposite direction.

# A Pure Faith

## Chapter 14

Miracles don't require huge faith—just a pure and simple faith. When the disciples asked Jesus to increase their faith, He responded very much the same as in Mark 11.

**"And the apostles said unto the Lord, Increase our faith. And the Lord said, If ye had faith as a grain of mustard seed, ye might say unto this sycamine tree, Be thou plucked up by the root, and be thou planted in the sea; and it should obey you"** (Luke 17:5-6).

In other words, Jesus was saying, "Guys, you don't need more faith. Your faith is sufficient. If your faith is only the size of a mustard seed, it's enough to uproot a tree without touching it. Just by speaking to it, you could make it leave." Then He continued, using the example of a slave:

**"But which of you, having a servant plowing or feeding cattle, will say unto him by and by, when he is come from the field, Go and sit down to meat? And will not rather say unto him, Make ready wherewith I may sup, and gird thyself, and serve me, till I have eaten and drunken; and afterward thou shalt eat and drink?"** (Luke 17:7-8).

Jesus was saying, "When you have a slave, you use them. The problem isn't that you don't have enough faith. It's the fact that you aren't using what you already have!" If you could understand this, it would answer some of the questions you've had like, "I know I believed, so why didn't it work?" It's not because you weren't believing; it's because you were believing and disbelieving at the same time!

The way you overcome your problem isn't by trying to get huge faith. If you believe that God heals, that's sufficient. If you believe that God heals, that's enough to see the dead raised—<u>IF</u> you don't submit to all of the negativism, doubt, and unbelief that comes from your senses.

## "This Kind"

**"And Jesus said unto them, Because of your unbelief: for verily I say unto you, If ye have faith as a grain of mustard seed, ye shall say unto this mountain, Remove hence to yonder place; and it shall remove; and nothing shall be impossible unto you. Howbeit this kind** [of unbelief] **goeth not out but by prayer and fasting"** (Matthew 17:20-21; brackets mine).

Traditionally, people have taught that this kind of "demon" only goes out by prayer and fasting. You'll hear people talk about how this is a "strong" demon. "It's a big problem, and we need to fast and pray before we deal with it. We also need to call the prayer chain because just one person isn't going to get this done. We'll need hundreds of people agreeing to be able to see this come out." Some people think that God is limited and if we ask Him for this, all the lights in heaven are going to dim. Not true!

This scripture is not saying that certain demons are stronger than others. Neither is it saying that certain demons won't respond to Jesus and faith in His name. "You also have to add fasting and prayer to it." That's not what this is talking about!

The subject of the sentence in verse 20 is unbelief. It was their unbelief that was the problem. Therefore, this kind of unbelief only goes out by prayer and fasting (Matthew 17:21). It doesn't take a huge faith—just a simple faith. However, there are some types of unbelief that are hard to deal with. You have to fast and pray to get them out.

# Ignorance, Wrong Teaching, and Natural

Unbelief can come from ignorance—lack of knowledge. Some people have never heard about miracles. They've never read the Bible. They were brought up in a natural world. They've been taught from the time they were a kid that the physical realm is all there is. They've been taught that there isn't a spiritual world or anything beyond the natural realm. That ignorance is unbelief, and it will hinder faith. You could come to that person and tell them about the Word of God, yet there will be a resistance just because they've never heard of or known this before. The antidote to this kind of unbelief is simply to tell them the truth. If they will embrace it over a period of time, the truth will set them free.

**"And ye shall know the truth, and the truth shall make you free"** (John 8:32).

The second type of unbelief is one that comes through wrong teaching. It's not a lack of knowledge, but wrong knowledge. I was brought up in this. I was taught that miracles passed away with the apostles and that God doesn't do them today. That's the kind of wrong teaching that made me resistant to miracles and believing God for them.

The antidote for this is the same—telling them the truth. Now, ignorance is easier to overcome than wrong teaching (a.k.a. disbelief). You have to get the wrong teaching out and then start the process of embracing the right teaching. It's more difficult, but it's basically the same process. You tell someone the truth and it will set them free if they believe it.

But the third kind of unbelief—natural unbelief—comes through your five senses. It was this type of natural unbelief that Jesus was talking about in the case of this demonized boy.

**"Then Jesus answered and said, O faithless and perverse generation, how long shall I be with you? how long shall I suffer you? bring him hither to me. And Jesus rebuked the devil; and he departed out of him: and the child was cured from that very hour. Then came the disciples to Jesus apart, and said, Why could not we cast him out? And Jesus said unto them, Because of your unbelief: for verily I say unto you, If ye have faith as a grain of mustard seed, ye shall say unto this mountain, Remove hence to yonder place; and it shall remove; and nothing shall be impossible unto you. Howbeit this kind goeth not out but by prayer and fasting"** (Matthew 17:20-21).

When they brought this boy to Jesus, he fell to the ground, wallowed, and foamed at the mouth.

**"And they brought him unto him: and when he saw him, straightway the spirit tare him; and he fell on the ground, and wallowed foaming"** (Mark 9:20).

Apparently these disciples had seen demons cast out before, but they hadn't seen a manifestation quite like this. Their senses—what they saw and heard—began giving them thoughts, feelings, and emotions contrary to what God had promised them.

The Lord had said, "You can cast out devils. I give you power over all demons."

**"And when he had called unto him his twelve disciples, he gave them power against unclean spirits, to cast them out, and to heal all manner of sickness and all manner of disease"** (Matthew 10:1).

**"Then he called his twelve disciples together, and gave them power and authority over all devils, and to cure diseases"** (Luke 9:1).

The disciples spoke, but what they saw and heard made it look like this demon wasn't going to respond. So they had unbelief come through their senses. They had faith, which is why they spoke and were perplexed about not seeing the healing come to pass, but they were still too sensitive to their physical senses.

## Sixth Sense

Your five senses aren't evil. God gave them to you for good things. You need your five physical senses to function in this world. It's hard to get around if you can't see. If you were to take me somewhere in your car, I'd want you to be able to go by what you see. I wouldn't want you to drive by faith. I'd want you to use your five senses!

However, at times God will call on all of us to do things that are contrary to our five physical senses. When the Lord calls on you to do something that counters your five senses, how will you respond? The answer to that question depends largely upon your relationship with God. Have you been spending time with Him, specifically in prayer and fasting? You need to spend time receiving from the spirit realm. This way, you will develop your "sixth sense." Then your mind can be trained to respond to faith the same way it responds to your five senses.

## Train Your Mind

**"But strong meat belongeth to them...who by reason of use have their senses exercised to discern both good and evil"** (Hebrews 5:14).

Your five senses can be exercised to discern things beyond just their physical, natural ability. You can get to where you develop this sixth sense of faith. If someone is blind, does that mean that they are just paralyzed and can't move, that they don't do anything because they can't see where they're going? No! They start learning to depend on their other senses more: what they can smell, feel, and hear. They'll use a cane or a seeing-eye dog to get around. They'll memorize a route through the house. Their mind will compensate for the lack of sight by depending even more on their other senses.

If you spend time with the Lord in fasting and prayer, you can train your mind to respond to faith. If you spend a lot of time with the Lord, you'll start seeing miracles. You'll see God deliver you in some way or another. You'll start hearing from God and have evidence of the reality of the spiritual world. You'll have physical proof that the Word of God works and over a period of time, faith will become like a sixth sense to you.

So, even if you can't physically perceive something that is consistent with what you're believing for, your mind can be trained to say, "Well, I can't see, taste, hear, smell, or feel it, but I've spent so much time with the Lord and seen Him come through on so many occasions, that I'm aware there is more." That's this sixth sense. You can get to where you rely on faith, just like a blind man relies on his hearing and feeling to still be mobile and get around. You can get to where you aren't limited to your five senses, but it doesn't happen easily.

# Exercise Yourself
## Chapter 15

**"But strong meat belongeth to them that are of full age, even those who by reason of use have their senses exercised to discern both good and evil"** (Hebrews 5:14).

Notice that Hebrews 5:14 says that their senses were exercised "by reason of use." In other words, you have to exercise. This word "exercise" is very important. You don't just get up and start preparing for a marathon the morning of the race. I actually trained for a marathon once and I didn't even make it. I ran half a marathon—thirteen point one miles—and it took me nearly a year to prepare to do that! People who prepare for, run in, and win marathons train for multiple years to get there. You can't start training the morning of the race. You have to exercise yourself!

Many Christians don't really spend much time with God. They live in the physical realm, working a job and watching television. They do everything in the natural realm, spending virtually no time praying and fellowshipping with God or fasting and denying their senses. Then they get into some crisis situation and give it all they have. They're 100 percent sincere and genuinely dedicated, but it's too little too late. They haven't exercised themselves. Some people even die, not because they were believing wrong, but because their senses had too much control over them.

This is why fasting works. Fasting is simply a denying of our five senses. Our taste or appetite is one of the strongest senses we have. People have actually murdered over food. I remember reading a story once about a group of people who were on their way west to California in the 1800s and ran into a blizzard. The children ate their mothers. They found them cannibalizing their own kin because of this desire for food. It's a strong, strong desire, and it doesn't take very long before it manifests. If you're someone who is just dominated and controlled by your five senses, if they are more real to you than what God says, and if that sixth sense of faith isn't the strongest, most dominant sense you have, then fasting is how you can change that.

## Who's Controlling Who?

Within just a few hours of when you start fasting, your appetite will begin complaining and trying to regain control. It will try to dominate and force you to eat. If you stick with it and say, "Nope, I'm going to believe God. Man does not live by bread alone, but by every word that proceeds from the mouth of God" (Matthew 4:4) and if that's your attitude and you persist, your body will rebel. It will try to control you.

If you just continue saying, "Well then, I'm going to fast all day," your appetite will respond, "All day? I'll be dead by evening!"

You answer, "Alright, we'll go two days," to which your body replies, "No, I'll never last two days!"

"Alright, three days!"

Pretty soon, your appetite will learn that it's going to survive, so it will have to submit. When you fast over a prolonged period of time, after about two or three days of denying your appetite, you actually reach a place to where you aren't hungry anymore. It doesn't bother you. You can get to a place to where you aren't missing it anymore, because your appetite is under control.

Then if sickness attacks your body, you can say, "I'm healed in the name of Jesus." If your body doesn't instantaneously manifest that healing and you're still in pain, you can tell your body "I'm not going by what I feel." If you've been fasting and praying—denying yourself and spending time in the presence of God—you've trained yourself to say, "What I believe is just as real as what I see, taste, hear, smell, and feel." Your body will respond to that. You'll be able to go on, stay the course, and stand until you see the manifestation of your healing.

But if you haven't been spending time in the spiritual realm, if you've just been totally occupied and dominated by the physical realm and you say, "Body, you're healed. I don't care what you feel. By the stripes of Jesus I was healed," your senses will answer, "Who are you to tell me anything? I tell you when to eat, what to eat, and how much to eat." Since you haven't exercised your senses, they'll control you instead of you controlling them.

## Sensitized to God

You can't avoid this natural type of unbelief that comes from what you see, taste, hear, smell, and feel. That's not an ignorance problem. It's not a renewing your mind problem. It's just a problem that you are spending more time in the physical world than you are in the spiritual world. You have to reverse that. You must get to where you are focused on the Lord and His Word.

When Peter was focused on Jesus, he didn't have any problems because he wasn't considering anything contrary to faith. But when he took his attention off of Jesus, he began to sink. Peter had already covered most of the distance. Jesus didn't have to run to him and grab him. The Lord just reached out and took hold of him. Peter was close enough that he could almost touch Jesus. Once he felt like he'd nearly made it, he relaxed! He took his attention off of the Lord and began to look at the wind and the waves. When he did that, he started sinking.

**"But when he saw the wind boisterous, he was afraid; and beginning to sink, he cried, saying, Lord, save me. And immediately Jesus stretched forth his hand, and caught him, and said unto him, O thou of little faith, wherefore didst thou doubt?"** (Matthew 14:30-31).

You can't afford to take your eyes off Jesus! Spend time in the Word, in prayer, denying your five senses, and fellowshipping with God. When you pray, your five senses are going to ask, "Who are you talking to? I can't see anybody. I can't hear anyone. I don't feel anybody here." But if you persist in prayer and relationship with God, you'll begin to experience miracles. There will be tangible proof that God is there and that He's talking to you. After a while, your senses will say, "Oh, there's another sense that I wasn't aware of. Whatever faith says is true" and you'll get to where your senses will bow and yield to faith. When you spend time in the presence of the Lord, your heart becomes sensitive to Him. It's just that simple!

Peter was able to walk on the water because he got out of the boat. He started walking to Jesus. As long as he kept his eyes on the Lord, he was fine. But once he took his eyes off Jesus, unbelief came. Peter still had faith, but unbelief started coming by his considering natural things.

All of us have natural things that are going to tell us that the Word of God doesn't work. If you can't see, taste, hear, smell, or feel it, your senses will try to convince you it doesn't exist. You are going to have to train and exercise yourself to know there's more to it than that. There is no way to do this except through spending quantity time in the presence of God through fasting and prayer.

## Go All the Way!

**"Howbeit this kind** [of unbelief] **goeth not out but by prayer and fasting"** (Matthew 17:21; brackets mine).

Prayer and fasting is the only way to deal with natural unbelief. You can get rid of the other two types of unbelief—ignorance and disbelief—just by hearing the truth and believing it. But the only way you can overcome your five senses and the unbelief they feed you is through fasting and prayer, spending time in God's presence. Be more at home in the spiritual world than you are in the physical. Get to where you believe that the spiritual world exists more than you believe what you can see, taste, hear, smell, and feel. You can exercise yourself to that, but it's going to take some time and effort. You can't wait until the morning of your trial to overcome this kind of unbelief. You just need to get focused on God and not look to the right or the left.

We let so much occupy us—television, radio, books, magazines—all kinds of things. In their place, they're okay. But when you are walking on water, you need to keep your eyes on Jesus. When you're out there believing God for a miracle, you can't afford to look to the right or to the left. You have to keep your eyes straight before you, not turned to either side. If you'll do that, not only can you be a water walker, but you can walk all the way to the other shore. You don't have to stop or fall. You can continue all the way to your God-ordained destination!

Your faith is sufficient. God gave you enough faith. It's not the fact that you have less than what you need. Actually you have more than what you need— more unbelief! Once you close the door on that unbelief, you will walk on water!

# Welcome to Your New Life!

Choosing to receive Jesus Christ as your Lord and Savior is the most important decision you'll ever make!

God's Word promises, **"That if thou shalt confess with thy mouth the Lord Jesus, and shalt believe in thine heart that God hath raised him from the dead, thou shalt be saved. For with the heart man believeth unto righteousness; and with the mouth confession is made unto salvation"** (Romans 10:9-10). **"For whosoever shall call upon the name of the Lord shall be saved"** (Romans 10:13).

By His grace, God has already done everything to provide salvation. Your part is simply to believe and receive.

Pray out loud, *"Jesus, I confess that You are my Lord and Savior. I believe in my heart that God raised You from the dead. By faith in Your Word, I receive salvation now. Thank You for saving me!"*

The very moment you commit your life to Jesus Christ, the truth of His Word instantly comes to pass in your spirit. Now that you're born again, there's a brand new you!

As His child, your loving heavenly Father wants to give you the supernatural power you need to live this new life.

**"For every one that asketh receiveth; and he that seeketh findeth; and to him that knocketh it shall be opened...how much more shall your heavenly Father give the Holy Spirit to them that ask him?"** (Luke 11:10-13).

All you have to do is ask, believe, and receive!

Pray, *"Father, I recognize my need for Your power to live this new life. Please fill me with Your Holy Spirit. By faith, I receive it right now. Thank You for baptizing me. Holy Spirit, You are welcome in my life!"*

Congratulations—now you're filled with God's supernatural power!

Some syllables from a language you don't recognize will rise up from your heart to your mouth. As you speak them out loud by faith, you're releasing God's power from within and building yourself up in the spirit (1 Corinthians 14:4, 14). You can do this whenever and wherever you like!

It doesn't really matter whether you felt anything or not when you prayed to receive the Lord and His Spirit. If you believed in your heart that you received, then God's Word promises you did. **"Therefore I say unto you, What things soever ye desire, when ye pray, believe that ye receive them, and ye shall have them"** (Mark 11:24). God always honors His Word—believe it!

Please contact me if you prayed either one or both of these prayers. I'd like to rejoice with you and send you a free gift that will help you understand and grow in your new relationship with the Lord. It's just my way of saying, *"Welcome to your new life!"*

# About the Author

For over four decades, Andrew Wommack has traveled America and the world teaching the truth of the Gospel. His profound revelation of the Word of God is taught with clarity and simplicity, emphasizing God's unconditional love and the balance between grace and faith. He reaches millions of people through the daily *Gospel Truth* radio and television programs, broadcast both domestically and internationally. He founded Charis Bible College in 1994 and has since established CBC extension schools in other major cities of America and around the world. Andrew has produced a library of teaching materials, available in print, audio, and visual formats. And, as it has been from the beginning, his ministry continues to distribute free audio materials to those who cannot afford them.

To contact Andrew Wommack please write, e-mail, or call:

Andrew Wommack Ministries, Inc.
P.O. Box 3333
Colorado Springs, CO 80934-3333
E-mail: awommack@aol.com
Helpline Phone (orders and prayer):
719-635-1111
Hours: 4:00 AM to 9:30 PM MST

Andrew Wommack Ministries of Europe
P.O. Box 4392
Walsall, WS1 9AR
England
E-mail: enquiries@awme.net
U.K. Helpline Phone (orders and prayer):
011-44-192-247-3300
Hours: 7:30 AM to 4:00 PM GMT

Or visit him on the Web at: www.awmi.net

# The Harrison House Vision

Proclaiming the truth and the power
Of the Gospel of Jesus Christ
With excellence;

Challenging Christians to
Live victoriously,
Grow spiritually,
Know God intimately.